True Christianity

Tanner Hnidey

True Christianity

by

Tanner Hnidey

Copyright © 2020

ISBN: 9798553946708

First Edition

Cover Design By: AlphaVision

Unless otherwise noted, all Scripture quotations are from the New International Version.

All rights reserved. No part of this publication may be reproduced or transmitted in any form or by any means, electronic or mechanical, including photocopy, recording, or any information storage retrieval system, without permission in writing from the copyright owner.

For my family: Mum, Dad, and Hunter.

Contents

Preface 1
The Conductor's Concerto 3
The Modern Habitation 12
The Hopeless Endeavor 25
The Law 35
The Necessary Qualification 51
The Married Bachelor – Part I 54
The Married Bachelor – Part II 65
The Temporary Reprieve 70
The Solution for the Enigma of Life 80
The Apex of Love 88
The Salvation of Man 96
The Sinner 110
The Surprised 116
The Substitute 120
The Saved 123
The Scared 126
The Secure 127
The Gradual Liberation 129
The Destiny of the Dead 142
The Ascension of the Alive and the Descension of the Divine 151
About the Author 160

Preface

The other day, I was reading, listening, and watching, some excerpts from a few of my favorite modern-day intellectuals whose contributions to society, I think, are extremely valuable. As I watched a particular discussion on life's meaning and purpose, my curiosity assumed control of my consciousness and I started to read viewer's comments pertaining to the discussion. The further I read, the more I realized just how many people, terribly desperate for even an ounce of hope in this cruel world, looked to these intellectuals and their ideas, as salvation.

But these hopeful listeners will soon find—I pray they have already found—that such wisdom will not result in the desired salvation, but damnation. This misplaced security is not damning because these ideas do not contain value, but because their very essence cannot provide salvation. The theories, commentaries, and arguments of these thinkers, compounded to create a doctrine that tries to make sense of existence, might delay the inevitable, but it will not save anyone from death.

In fact, the more this wisdom of the world is relied upon, the more an individual clings to it for hope, the quicker the doctrine, and subsequently the person, will crumble and deteriorate.

Therefore, I was compelled to write about the one Savior, one hope, and one path to everlasting life, Jesus Christ. He alone is the sacrifice for sin, he alone frees a person from death, and he alone is the eternal salvation for humanity. As such, this book is about Christ, and Christ alone, in the hope that you too, dear reader, might receive freedom from death and become a True Christian.

I

The Conductor's Concerto

The Conductor's cosmic composition of His concerto, called Creation, is undoubtedly the most magnificent stroke of brilliance ever. It is made all the more awe-inducing and jaw-dropping when the divine artist raises His baton and begins to conduct this grand symphony to produce finite phrases within the infinite melody of potential eternity. And this conductor begins the story of our reality by not just choosing the orchestra but by also *creating* them: the instruments they play, the stage on which they sit, and the music itself. He delegates their structure in a specific arrangement that is finely tuned and perfectly suited for the indivisible harmonies of life. The rich, full, and powerful basses of creation are situated at the back so as not to overpower the tenderness of the flutes. And the warm clarinets are not positioned next to the crisp, distinct flair of the trumpets. If the opposite were true, the orchestra would perform and sound disjointed, brash, and flat-out bad. In fact, it would be no orchestra at all, and the intended music would not be anything resembling beauty and order, but ugliness and chaos.

This perfect ensemble is also a symphony of mystery. Behind the golden curtain of glorification, the Conductor has reserved specific musicians and instruments that have not yet been revealed. Presently, we only know they exist, and that we will one day witness their part in the piece, because the Conductor has told us so. The nature of these ethereal musicians, their perfect pitch, melody, and harmony, is reserved for the resurrected man.

As I stated before, the Conductor carefully places His orchestra in a logical manner, designed only by Him to optimize every sound produced from His symphony. He hears every note and listens to every vibrato, and no chord of the universe passes through His ear undetected. But it is not enough to simply position His musicians in a manner He desires. This conductor's concert is His and His alone. He begins by constructing the concert hall with materials He made. Every reverb is analyzed, and every acoustic is accounted for. Brick by brick and board by board, He assembles it with the hands of a carpenter until a physical structure stands solitary in the realm of the metaphysical. In this hall lies all reality, both seen and unseen. Everything we know as real, and things we do not yet know, are contained in this gargantuan of space and time contingent upon His existence. Apart from the being who built it and what is contained in His heavenly realms, anything outside the theatre is not a "thing" at all.

The stage where the musicians are seated is crafted from abstracts that exist necessarily, such as the laws of mathematics and rationality. It is the foundation that, although silent, often unappreciated, and causally inert, is essential to ensure that the members are able to perform comprehensively.

Of course, the musicians and their instruments, like the basses and percussion, are the photons, atoms, molecules—the fundamental forces of the symphony and nature. They form the backbone of the universal orchestra. Without them, there is no stabilizing harmony and no universal rhythm for the design of the delicate instruments to anchor their melody upon.

The trumpets of His creation provide splashes of color. They are decorative and impossible to miss, things that primarily serve to enhance the beauty and spontaneity of creation. Planets and their diverse landscapes, stars of unfathomable size and their eventual supernovae, galaxies hundreds of thousands of lightyears in diameter and their respective local groups all serve their purpose in the grand design. For the elementary lay astronomer like myself, it is tempting to declare the cosmos the grandest of all God's creation. Apart from Christ, I see the existence of the Divinity most naturally on a clear moonless night in the country. But the ever-expanding expanse is minuscule in wonder compared to

His masterpiece, for the universe is not the pinnacle of this concert.

As He continues composing His score, He articulates the melody of life. Unlike the falsely perceived monotonous harmony that can sometimes appear to define the axioms of the cosmos (like the sun rising in the morning and setting in the evening), living things are spontaneous, quick, complex, and ever-changing. Trees, plants, and all animals serve to provide a most incredible variety to the sound of the spiritual symphony.

Then the Conductor gives the musicians their sheet music. The vast variety of notes, rhythms, and dynamics played individually are, although not wrong, incomplete and unsatisfactory. But, when each member plays their piece as part of the unification of all things from and through the conductor, life flourishes. One section does not perform in the key of B flat while another plays in A minor. The Earth cannot be as close to the sun as Mercury is, a round ball naturally rolls smoothly while a cube does not, and E does not equal mc^4, but mc^2.

The Conductor raises His baton and the musicians their instruments. Everyone is totally in tune with the Leader and is ready to play *exactly* what He desires. The first note is struck, and it is a sound so warm, so joyful, so lovely, that the likes of Beethoven, Mozart, and Bach could never recreate.

But wait. The Conductor turns around and stares at an empty theatre. There is no one to play for, no one to share His creation with apart from Himself. That is not to say He is lonely, only that He has no audience to enjoy His masterpiece. He is akin to the husband and wife who painted the guest room blue or pink, built a crib, purchased a car seat, and yet hold no child. This lack must be corrected, and it is remedied through the creation of the audience: *man.*

Humanity is the embodiment of the entire composition. God has commissioned this piece for mankind. Everything that has been created, from the largest wonder of the universe to the smallest particle, is for the human. We are interconnected with the soil, plants, and all Earth's inhabitants because we are made for it. "That's wonderful," you say, "but if that's all we are, then we are little more than dirt that has the capacity to think and reason and love."

Not at all. It is much more than that. We have been given the distinct and divine privilege of being made in the image of the Conductor, God. While we share traits with animals, such as blood carrying oxygen to organs, the necessity of water for life, emotional reactions to specific circumstances, and other common denominators, only humans claim legitimacy to the apex honor of being made in the image of God. And by "image of God," I mean precisely that—God looks at us and sees a reflection of Himself. You are I are not only declared good, but *very good*, because God sees a mirror of Himself in our persons. Although organisms, plants, and animals, live, only man has been given the privilege of *life*.

For a moment, disregard the sin that is presently within us. Flex your fingers and write down a thought on a page. In doing something as simple (though there is nothing simple about it) as that, the wonderful works of God are thoroughly manifested within you. Being able to interact with the world around you, commenting on what you believe as truth, exercising rational thought, and countless others abilities are all fundamental attributes of God.

Everything God creates, He does with a specific purpose. That purpose stamps His signature throughout the artwork of the universe. All creation serves as a portrait of the Triune God in one way or another. It is a perfect portrait of His likeness. The wonder of it all is that even though He is a being of infinite dimensions—and we only have a four-dimensional canvas with which to work—the picture of Himself in us is entirely corresponding to His nature.

The canvas that displays this picture of God's person is so vast that the Christian witnesses the Trinity every day. In nature, in scripture, in reality, and in all life, God is visible and evident, even to those who do not yet believe. Through the gentle flap of a butterfly, coupled with wings intricate in color, design, and symmetry, and thin as paper, I see a description of God's tenderness.

On a warm summer's day, I travel to the hills overlooking the valleys I once discovered as a child, and I am enshrouded in the peace of Heaven. As I sit on the porch during the rain, any thoughts or worries I have are silenced by the crack of thunder. Instead, I am forced to sit in reverent fear and contemplate the wonder of His mighty power. I reach the summit of the rocky mountain and find a meadow, hidden from the rest of the world. When it opens and reveals the flowers, grass, animals, and a secret lake guarded from prying eyes by a dense shield of the evergreens, how can I fail to see His meekness? There is serenity in His security.

Look up. Gaze at the stars. For a moment, contemplate the universe before you and be awestruck with the Almighty's infinite nature. The grandest star is little more than a grain of sand compared to the size of our Creator. The brilliance of the supernova is dull compared to His face, and the density of the neutron star is as light as air compared to the weight of my sin and yours that He bore on the cross for you and me.

Now, not only are we the esteemed audience of His symphony, with much joy, we even began to take part in conducting it. We are known intimately with the Divine and so the movements of God became our own. When His baton moved up, so did ours. When He flipped a page, so did we. By design, we became the designated rulers of Earth and heralds of God. All that we do, all that we are, is to assist in spreading the perfection of the One who created us. So then, we are much more than just an audience watching the Maestro at work. On the contrary, we are the family of the Sovereign Supreme.

The symphony commences, and no harmony has ever sounded so sweet. The melody is genius unrivalled and all is according to perfection. Then, the most remarkable transformation occurs. Though we are created to enjoy and help conduct the music, we become part of the divine notes. The flutes of the symphony flutter, and we discover ourselves falling in love. A child is conceived and the trumpets flare to announce a regal celebration. Life is full of crescendos and swells as we travel ever nearer to the Infinite. There are times of tenderness when the music is nearly imperceptible and times of excitement when the soundwaves of emotion make us grasp onto something for stability. In fact, without man, the piece ceases to be God's score at all.

But after a while, we mistakenly began to believe that we *alone* could conduct the symphony of our lives. In an act of love, the original Conductor allowed Himself to be replaced when the audience staged a coup and seized command of the symphony under the "progressive" notion of modern moral and spiritual evolution. The orchestra is now horribly out of tune, the melody is compromised, and the harmony is destroyed. What has followed is chaos, evil, and death.

II

The Modern Habitation

Upon contemplation of scripture, there seems to be a grand, overarching, understanding that the story of human life is characterized by a tale of *two* spiritual cities. To try and grasp this concept, I am currently imagining a flat, metaphysical plane. On one side of the plane, I see the "City of Righteousness," and on the other, separated by a "wilderness" of wild space, I see the "City of Sin." We all, as beings created in the image of God, are fundamentally interconnected with this plane. That is to say, an individual can either be a citizen of the City of Righteousness or a citizen of the City of Sin. Put simply then, when I say "city," all I mean is that an individual can serve God or not.

Just as a person can live in harmony with another, if a person serves, loves, and has faith in God, they "live" in the City of Righteousness. All believers who inhabit it are ruled by the Lord and experience peace, joy, love, hope, and life. Their inward spirit and, as a product of that spirit, their outward actions will reflect the King of that city, God. As we will discuss later, in our original creation and before we rebelled against God, humanity was intended to live in this city forever. But because we sinned against our King and because God cannot cohabit with sin, we were required to travel across the wilderness of this plane and live in the other city, the City of Sin. Before I describe the City of Sin, I must say that any person can certainly be brought back to loving Him and returning to Righteousness, but this can only be done through the salvation of Christ.

Now, like the City of Righteousness, the City of Sin is also ruled by a spiritual being. But He is not God. Instead, He is a being, who we shall describe later, called Satan. And, because Satan rules as a tyrant, I think it is appropriate to call him an "emperor." If an individual resides in this city, as we all initially do because of our sin, they do not serve God. And, similar to those who serve God, the inward spirit of a non-believer will manifest itself through their outward actions.

And this prison—although we self-appointed gods still prefer the term "City of Sin"—we now inhabit was not our original home. We did not always serve what is evil! On the contrary, when we were created, living with God was our perfected mansion.

The act of spiritually serving God was diligently and joyfully manifested physically in the real Garden of Eden. Think of this Garden as the municipality within the greater region of Eden where the City of Righteousness was located. That is to say, the Garden of Eden is where we served God. Eden was a paradise, and although a Canadian vacationing in the Bahamas to escape negative 40-degree temperatures might disagree with me, it was not a paradise because of its geographical location. Eden was not a paradise because of the vibrant trees which adorned the landscape, or because of the rich rivers that supplied the garden with fresh water, or because of the lion resting with the lamb, or because of the warm sun. No, Eden was a paradise because paradise is not a place but a *person*. Eden was a paradise because it was there that God assumed the form of man and walked with Adam and Eve.

Each day, the couple sought refuge in holiness as they talked with God as their Father and as their Friend. Indeed, it is better to live in a hut with family who loves you dearly than a mansion alone. In doing so, the hut becomes a mansion, and the mansion a hut. Of course, I am not implying that Eden was a hut, but only that it was designated a mansion because of *Who* was there, not *what* was there.

While residing in this City of Righteousness and engaging in the work God had for us, there were numerous jobs that required attending. Modern tasks, even those easily drudged down into the depths of boredom by the anchor of the imperfect and the mundane, become tolerable and perhaps amusing with the company of family and friends all working together while making jokes and appreciating each other's common passion for the topic. An equation of algebra that is difficult and painstaking to solve is made enjoyable with the inclusion of like-minded students and classmates. The same is true of farmers harvesting in a field or marketing professionals brainstorming in an office. How much more exciting and fulfilling were jobs in the City of Righteousness where all was perfect and evil was absent!

Now the Almighty, to create the necessary conditions for perfect love, placed in Eden that now-infamous Tree of Knowledge of Good and Evil.[1] The mere thought of trying to exalt oneself above God would most certainly have constituted a sinful state. But through the Tree, humanity was given a physical command so that, if a human spirit decided to exalt himself greater than God, it would be realized through eating from the Tree of Knowledge of Good and Evil. Certainly, Adam and Eve were *not* sinful before they ate from the Tree. On the contrary, Adam and Eve were perfect when they were created, and they were given the free will to love God or not. It is with the creation, and subsequent command to not eat the fruit from the Tree of Knowledge of Good and Evil that this free will could be practiced.

But before we continue, it is important to understand that evil (otherwise known as sin) is not a

---

[1] Genesis 2:17

creation but an absence and a failure. By definition, sin is the absence of God and the degree by which we fall short of His glory. Specifically, it is the absence of good, which is the absence of God, because God *is* good. It's not a small absence either; it's infinite. This is the degree that we are absent of righteousness when we sin. For if sin is to be void of God, and God is infinite, then you and I are naturally void of the infinite in our sinful state. Of course, only the Infinite Himself can bridge that chasm, for nothing finite can possibly repair an eternal gap.

In commanding the innocent couple in the Garden, "You shall not eat from this tree or you will surely die," God really said, "If you become prideful in your heart and place yourself above Me, you will eliminate My indwelling presence within you. But I am life. If you eliminate Me, you *must* die in order to uphold the logical reality of My nature and yours. As physical proof of spiritual transgression, this sin of pride will be actualized by consuming the fruit from the tree I have commanded you not to eat. Therefore, if you sin, you can never possess any merit in accusing Me of unjustly fulfilling this law. You may never justly gnash your teeth at Me and say, 'You didn't properly judge my spirit! I never put my soul above You.' For a sinful heart will be revealed by eating the fruit from the Tree of Knowledge of Good and Evil. But remember, you do not need to eat from that tree! I have made you perfect! Trust in Me, and follow

My commands, and evil will be an unknown reality for you."

So, placing the Tree of Knowledge of Good and Evil in the Garden of Eden was not a temptation, nor was it a guarantee of eventual damnation, but it was, perhaps, the beginning of our salvation.

The walls that surrounded the City of Righteousness where our mansions were housed, sustained, and defended by the eternity of God, were impenetrable. Overseen by innumerable legions of warrior angels and protected by the Everlasting Divinity, what enemy would possess the unthinkable tactical insolence required to order their divisions to storm the city by force? Who would dare attack the children of God as they are serving Him?

Ah, but Satan is a brilliant strategist and was furious with God's command that angelic beings would serve humans. But he knew that the hearts of Adam and Eve, perhaps curious about the landscape beyond the realm of the wonderful, could be corrupted. What brings a loving parent, in this case, God, more misery and sadness then having their children rebel against them? Indeed, it may have been that Satan's initial rebellion was his deception of Adam and Eve. Perhaps his fall was simultaneous with ours.

With regards to this "Satan" we call "emperor," It ought not be controversial to state that he is a being of pure evil. But he was not created that way. On the contrary, he was created as a perfectly righteous spiritual servant of the Divine. But because of his rebellion, without external temptation, he is now the beautiful adversary, but not the equal of God. And it is a mistake to assume that Satan is a frightening figure. It is natural for individuals to flee from that which is horrifically scary and intends to do them harm. Yet we are drawn to Satan and his public, but manipulated, appearance. Caesar was adored by the Roman people. Crowds flocked to Lenin, and spectators cheered for Mussolini. No, Satan is not frightening, but enticing. He masquerades as something wonderful, a promise without any substance. He does not look fearful, but he is to be feared.

As was alluded to in the previous paragraph, originally, the emperor was a cherubim, a created servant of God named Lucifer. Lucifer's perfect heart and his entire nature was glorious. And yet, with his sinful rebellion against God, he began to see himself as so beautiful that he could look, care, and focus on nothing but himself. He thought himself so marvelous that, in his own eyes, he was fit for worship. His Empire of Evil, the City of Sin that he rules, was created in the instant of his corruption—a kingdom of the self in direct opposition to the kingdom of the Triune. His wickedness knows no bounds, and his tactics are meticulously designed and implemented for each individual of the Earth, including you.

For the sensitive personality, Satan might attack with harsh words of accusations and fell his prey into crippling depression as they long for their mental affliction to terminate. For others, Satan may charge as a beast and overflow their lives with physical misery. Perhaps this evil emperor whispers words of false comfort into the ear of one who is contemplating their evil nature in order to lull them to Hell under a false sense of security in good deeds. Nonetheless, no matter what strategy he utilizes, he is always a roaming lion without a home seeking to rip his prey to shreds under the scorching sun of sin.

To infiltrate the human heart and initiate the now-infamous fall of man, Satan knocked on the their door, not brandishing a sword in his hand, but holding a box, crafted with the ratio of Fibonacci—of promised riches. Everything about its presentation was appealing. Unlocked by the key of disobedience, the box opened and revealed photos and descriptions of a new enlightened city, brighter and more brilliant than the one God had made. As the great defenses of intelligence and wisdom were willfully surrendered, this smooth-talking salesman pitched the pleasures of knowledge of right and wrong to Eve (and most probably to Adam).

"Did God *really* say that you cannot eat from any tree in the Garden of Eden?" Satan smoothly asks.

To which Eve replies, "Oh no. We can eat the fruit from any tree we want in the entirety of Eden as long as we don't eat from the Tree of Knowledge of Good and Evil. If we do, then Adam and I will die."

"I see. What if I told you that you could gain all the knowledge that God has? If you eat from that tree, you will know right from wrong and become as wise as the Divine. Yes, that is my offer: eat from the Tree and you will gain more knowledge and power than you could possibly imagine. You will become *like* God."

"I could be, couldn't I? I have no more need for this law. The fruit of iniquity looks refreshing to my spiritual eye. I can become the master of my fate."

As the human heart began to swell with pride, the prospect of becoming independent looked more than just appealing; it seemed necessary. An act of instant rebellion derived eternal consequences. The newly created spirit of pride, "I will make my thyself a god," actualized its spiritual wickedness through consuming of fruit from the Tree of Knowledge of Good and Evil.

Sin!

First Eve, then Adam, and with Adam came the fall of the physical world. For man is intrinsically interconnected with the Earth. Our enemy deceived us and sacked our City of Righteousness. We were supposed to spread the wonder of life in Eden throughout the wilderness of the Earth. Instead, we spread nothing but sin and death. That powerful lion now grasps our heads between his jaw. Our spiritual jugular was severed, and our neck crushed under the unbearable pressure of death.

But what was sinful about the tree? Was there poison in its fruit, or did its sap contain the elixir of evil? Not at all. Granted, this Tree of Knowledge of Good and Evil was holy, because it was set apart for a specific purpose, but I do not believe scripture describes it as possessing magical powers or mystical properties. Perhaps nothing about it was peculiar in appearance or design except that God commanded, "You shall not eat from this particular tree." God could have commanded us not to touch a specific tiger in the garden, or not to drink water in a certain way, or to not do a somersault, but He chose to use a very symbolic figure in the Bible: a tree. This means that the sin was *not* the act of Eve's neurons firing through her synapses, communicating to the muscles in her arm and hand to reach up and grab a piece of fruit, then bringing the food to her mouth, and finally consuming the fruit. That process of events are mere actions, and sin is not an action. Therefore, the sin was her disobedience against God. That particular sin originated in the heart, was derived from pride, and merely actualized through the eating of the fruit. Adam and Eve did not believe God and His word, and God rightfully credited their actions as unrighteousness.

This reality is why you and I are naturally dead. Through Adam, acting as a proxy for mankind, all of humanity from the ancient of time to the end of days is deemed to be void of God and, therefore, sinful creatures.[2]

---

[2] 1 Corinthians 15:22

You might counter this argument by saying, "But Adam and Eve did not die, at least not instantly, and I am not presently dead either."

And in one sense, you are correct only if "death" is defined as the expiration of the temporal body's animation of the individual spirit. In that sense, if you are reading this, you're not physically dead. Granted, even if you are healthy, with each passing second the oxygen you breathe slowly rusts the iron in your blood, bringing you one second closer to that physical death that all people fear. Nonetheless, what I am articulating was the *spiritual and physical separation from God,* that is, death, that occurred at the moment of the fall. Spiritually and physically, our connection with the Divine, who brought us into existence, was instantly broken at the moment of original sin. Cut off from the Godhead and now suffering under the rule of Satan, we have died to righteousness and are now evil.

The reluctant march out of God's city and into the Empire of Evil was embarrassing and lonely. Granted, as we beheld the City of Sin, we were greeted with a capitol made of pure gold. That is to say, the prospect of rejecting God and sinning is always enticing. Billboards depicted lavish lifestyles of sensual pleasure and material goods. The gardens of wonder and architecture of pomp were constructed outside this new abode of sin were supposed to foreshadow the fulfillment and beauty to come.

But then we enter this new city, and all is not as it seemed. Misery overtakes our countenance as we realize the City of Sin is not what the brochures led us to believe. The promised beauty is a projection, an illusion, and a lie. The buildings of this new empire are decrepit and dilapidated. The "art" is crude and objectified, morality appears to be subjective, and an unspoken noose of nihilism hangs in the air. Where there is supposed to be pleasure, there is pain. Where there is supposed to be love, there is lust. Where there is supposed to be splendor, there is suffering and sorrow. But there is no need to continue to attempt to describe this new dwelling, for you and I already know its attributes.

"Turn around! Run away! Go back!"

But it is too late. The guards at the sin gate *kindly* hand out mandatory blinders. Put them on, and reality becomes distorted with everything appearing lovely and fine, promoting the self-reassuring statement with a crack in the voice, "Yes, I have chosen this, and it is excellent."

III

The Hopeless Endeavor

But of course, reality can only be manipulated for so long. The blinders, constructed from the doctrine of self-help books and prosperity gospels, seek to convince you that all is well. But the more they are relied upon the faster they fade and eventually disintegrate into dust. The mansions of the Empire of Sin begin to look like the slums they are, and the gardens gradually reveal themselves to be graveyards. True, if man is the measure of all things, then this horror is subjective, and humanity as a whole cannot declare them to be objectively bad. For example, in Stalin's commitment to advancing the satanic doctrine of communism, he seemed to marinate in the blood of tens of millions slaughtered at his command. In his eyes, if his power was consolidated, then the gulags, the starvation, and the death of the forgotten was "good."

But we thank God because man is not the supreme moral judiciary. Nonetheless, as the starving search for food and as the physicist scours for answers uniting quantum theory and general relativity, the soul cries for eternal satisfaction. In a desperate effort to appease the continual hunger pains of the spirit and to explain its purpose and reason, humanity embarks on a mission to achieve fulfilment, not confined to just the world, but searching through the entire universe. Things that are by no means bad in and of themselves, like money, power, fame, self-betterment, fitness, and even family, are all sought after to quench the thirst of contentment and peace. Of course, to try and quench the thirst for purpose with such material things is like drinking saltwater. Money will inflate and plummet with its arbitrary value, power will be lost, the fit will grow old and become frail, the physically beautiful will relinquish their looks, and family will die.

Seemingly paradoxical, our pride is exalted when we bow to a god, so long as it's not the one true God. The demonstration of bowing to a self-created god—which by definition is no god at all—is really the act of capitulating to the desires of our own heart. Therefore, the created god is not something like money, alcohol, phones, or actual idols. It is also not immaterial entities like lust, greed, or anger. The god you worship is *you*. In serving a god, you are serving your individual pride, thereby exalting pride, which is the exaltation of self. You are praised and your pleasures indulged, because who dares challenge our supposed inherent right to exercise sovereignty over ourselves? <u>The answer is only our natural enemy to our sin nature: Jesus Christ</u>.

However the one who thinks they are free to engage in the desires of their heart is not really "free" at all. Instead such a person is a slave to sin, bowing before the cravings of their secular spirit. In fact, in bowing before yourself, you are actually bowing before the emperor of evil, Satan. Why? Because Satan commands us to bow to ourselves. He even tempted Jesus Christ to do so![3] Therefore, in bowing to our pride, we are actually obeying the orders of the emperor of sin.

More than that, although we pride ourselves in acting under our own volition and living like a god, we are careful to relinquish responsibility for actions that produce immediate undesirable consequences. Instead, we chalk these instances up to "fate, destiny, and dumb luck." To illustrate my point, suppose you decide to indulge in the temptation of greed by gambling at a casino. After winning a few rounds at the roulette table, your conscience persuades you to "play a few more times." Why not? After all, you have been winning. Why not live free and ride the hot hand? Addicted to the rush of adrenaline initiated by high-stakes chance (though there is no such thing as a small stake) and satisfied with the flood of dopamine that is rewarded in winning, the

---

[3] Matthew 4:1-11

City of Sin flashes bright and beautiful for a moment. And then it's gone. If you lose your money, the consequences are clear and well documented. But even if you leave the casino a winner, you have not won anything of spiritual value, and that is the only value that is worth anything at all in the eternal run. Is there no shame for a man prepared to gamble his child's education fund away for one dollar more? Like Spurgeon said, "A young gambler is sure to make an old beggar if he lives long enough." No, in every scenario, the City of Sin returns to the wasteland we know it to be. This perceived "freedom" is nothing more than slavery to the self, and slavery to self is slavery to sin. If the high of a particular pleasure ceases, the sin is repeated in an attempt to reintroduce euphoria and the nourishment the heart craves. It will fail.

It will fail because placing hope in such pleasures is treasonous against God and therefore is a betrayal of His being. It is very terrible to be betrayed by someone—gut-wrenching if it is by someone whom you love and thought loved you. Yet to be betrayed is not a sin, merely tragic. To *be* the betrayer, however, is one of the highest forms of evil. It determines that the betrayed, an image-bearer of God, is unworthy to be treated as he deserves. Satan betrayed God, adulterers betray families and sacred oaths under God, and man, in his rejection of Christ, commits the unforgivable and betrays the Holy Spirit.

If, in an effort to quiet the conscience and justify the action, the betrayer simultaneously chooses to accuse the betrayed of betrayal, the betrayer betrays the betrayed yet again. This betrayer then summits to the apex of all sinful betrayal when the betrayed is the infinite, perfect, Creator. And if the Creator truly is infinite in His existence, nature, person, power, glory, might, love, and mercy, then punishment for sin cannot be a year in Hell, a "lower" spot in Heaven, a purgatory period of pain post-post-mortem, or ceasing to exist at all. It must be equivalent to the depth of the betrayal. In reality, payment for such treason must be of an infinite duration in order to necessarily satisfy the eternal requirement of the righteous law.

But our pride tells us, "Never mind that now. Set aside and forget the consequences of betrayal. Our tempter of sin, Satan, reminds us that we possess our kingdom and we must rule. So let's get on with it."

Our conscience might, at least for a little while until its flame is nearly snuffed out, reply, "Ah, but remember the terrible feeling of being pierced by those eyes of pure fire that reveal the motives of our soul. Remember our continual charges against our Creator while feeling that overwhelming sense of shame. Remember the heartbreaking sorrow of being cast out of the City of Righteousness into the wasteland of sin located in this barrenness of Earth. Listen to His continual call home though we are disgraced."

"Enough!" shouts our pride. "None of that matters now. You are not a slave to this superstition known as Satan, but you are a "master of your own fate" and sovereign over your own realm. A self-proclaimed king or queen like yourself never bows to another, especially not a foreign enemy trying to invade your personal dominion."

Left to his own volition, man descended from Adam will never, can never, yield to the peace freely offered by God. The attempts of reconciliation by the King of the City of Righteousness are always greeted with hostility and disdain lest the empire we serve be decimated to dirt. This ideology cumulates in the affirmation of man saying, "I should rather rule in misery than serve with joy."

Our natural inclination to vehemently reject the goodness of God is amplified, very brilliantly, by the strategic actions of the emperor. To understand these fundamental strategies, let us examine two separate tactics in their most fundamental form. Granted, we are oversimplifying this analysis to its logical limit, but for the purpose of this brief account, it'll do. Bear in mind, Satan may utilize any combination and ratio of these two strategies. Each cup of damnation is specifically prescribed for the individual, and Satan is devious in his efforts to ensure we take our medicine. But for simplicity, for now, let us briefly explain them as they are in their purest forms.

The Hopeless Endeavor

The first strategy Satan utilizes to deceive us into rejecting the goodness of God is to fill the aesthetically pleasing drink of death in a golden cup of elegance. Joy, laughter, wealth, love, and other flavors are vigorously combined to form a delicious concoction. From the perspective of the exiled observer, the citizens of the City of Sin are often happy by all outward appearances. The grass always looks greener across the fence. The acquisition of money, fame, power, beauty, prestige, and other neutral attributes seem, at least to the one who desires such things, to guarantee fulfillment. Coupled with observations of sinful men enjoying what is intrinsically good, like friends having each other for dinner parties and scientists discussing the nature of the quantum realm over a cup of coffee, one would be rightfully inclined to believe that this life of rejecting God is "good."

But it only takes a drop of poison to kill a man. Satan, ensuring the drink is thoroughly diluted with the sweetness of God's attributes, masks the bitter drop of death until it's too late. A sweet drink needs no more sugar; a happy soul in sin needs no Savior.

Satan must be doubly cautious with this second approach, because man is never nearer to faith in the person of Christ than when he has lost hope in everything else. The opposite tactic then to encourage rejection of God's goodness is to fill a dirty cup with poison and nothing but poison. An individual's entire life may be dominated by real or perceived suffering, depression, and eventual nihilism with only periodic glances of hope and joy. Remember that the man's life may be rather blessed compared to other parts of the world, but Satan only requires the man's mind to think no one is worse off than he. The drink is so bitter and so vile to taste that no ingredient appears to be able to merely sweeten, let alone eliminate, its foul taste. There is little that is more tragic than a life such as this, but the outcome is the same as all others—death. Whether it is a drop of poison, a shot of poison, or an entire glass of poison, death is the consequence of sin.

But again, our pride is quick to remind the sinner that there is no need to contemplate the dismal reality of death. Being kings and queens of our own empire, it is better to focus on ruling. And to rule properly, one requires soldiers to defend interests and attack any enemies. But of course, each individual has their own little empire, but it is merely an empire of self—like every other sovereign within the city. The king or queen of self has no servants to fight on their behalf, because any prospective servants are too busy serving themselves in their own kingdoms. Therefore, when Satan sounds the alarm of war, the only course of action is for the individual to arm himself or herself personally, dress in their battle garments, and prepare to fight.

As a sinner—king or queen turned soldier of Hell's empire—you beautifully adorn yourselves in armor of

The Hopeless Endeavor

accolades, greaves of material stability, shields of university degrees, swords of monetary success, and a helmet of worldly wisdom. As you continue to convince yourself that this fight is your free choice, you carefully choose the colors of armor to elevate yourself as unique and distinguished above the other rulers on the battlefield—although you will find it peculiar that, irrespective of prior communication, every soldier ends up deciding to wear the same color. Your enemy, those wretched men and women who left the City of Sin and never returned home, are not dressed as grandiose and eloquent as you are. They left a kingdom of material riches and abundant pleasure for a kingdom of a meek spiritual life, and it shows. In fact, their armor appears rather pathetic, if non-existent. They do not dress themselves with their individual intelligence or drape their being in worldly accomplishments. It seems like they do not care about their protection at all.

The enemy, the Christian, does not see you in the same way you see yourself. In fact, these Christians do not even see themselves in the same way you see them. In their view, their outward appearance and yours are inconsequential. They are too busy focusing on the name, nature, and very person that is their Commander to be concerned with their own countenance, appearance, and possessions. When this kingdom soldier of righteousness sees a soldier of the sinner's empire, they look beyond the realm of the finite of accomplishments.

The soldier of righteousness does not behold an enemy legion of beautifully adorned, yet intimidating, soldiers, but an army of tragic oppression—of hopeless slaves dressed in despair, driven hard by their master, chained to their emperor, and led around like a dog on a leash.

"Pay no attention to them," dismisses your pride. "They know nothing of your good works that you initiate under your own volition."

After the battle, you march back and see the City of Sin. "Ah! There it is! Look at my city and the gold and the gardens!"

Of course, you pass through the gates and, finding the city's condition to be the same—if not worse—from when you left it, the blinders return to their rightful place hooked on your ears and perched on your nose. For a while, everything is well again.

The Commander of the other army, observing this phenomenon and all the abuse these people endure, tells His followers that the kings and queens of the empire have ceased to be enemies and are instead the tired, weary, and lost, all in desperate need of a Savior.

IV

The Law

I previously told you that every human descended from Adam is a sinner. In fact, I would be comfortable to define humanity, very rudimentarily, as being a descendent of Adam. In metaphorical terms, I am declaring that scripture states that all of us are born into the City of Sin. Yet our previous chapter assumed a position that transcended the sinner. If I am a citizen of sin, how do I know that sin and sinful actions are *bad*? Or, if I was a citizen of sin, what enlightened me and allowed me to escape the city's apparently unescapable walls?

To put it another way, we recognize a possible contention that states to the Christian, "You are assuming that these 'sinful actions' are wrong. Perhaps they are not. If you suppose that my nature is evil and we therefore naturally engage in evil, how do you or I know that what I do is wrong? Is evil not a subjective term?

How do I prove that evil exists? How can you prove that I do evil at all? I know you define evil to be the absence of God. But if God is absent, how am I to know that He is absent? If a child is born blind, he does not understand the concept of light. How can I understand the concept of righteousness?"

Such a question is legitimate. Pretend, for a moment, that across the vast expanse of the cosmos, there is a planet called Orangeopolis. The atmosphere is created in such a way that only the orange spectrum of visible light is permitted through. Therefore, everything in and on this planet is orange. The star that warms the planet is orange, the trees are orange, the bananas are orange, the mountains are orange, the snow is orange, and the grain is orange.

On Orangeopolis, there is a species of primitive humanoids who traverse the world. They are competent in reading and speaking their dialect, but not much else. They have not conducted scientific studies of their world or of what lies beyond their system.

Suppose I send these beings a message that states, "Come to the planet Earth and see the crystal blue water."

These humanoids who reside on Orangeopolis cannot comprehend the color blue, because all they have ever understood is the color orange. The word "blue" would mean as much to them as calculus does to a donkey, because blue exists apart from the known reality

The Law

of Orangeopolis. Of course, in sending the message, I am implying that *I* know that the color blue exists, what it is, and what its properties are, even if I do not understand everything about light. I am assuming a position separate from Orangeopolis. In witnessing the color blue, I ascend the reality of Orangeopolis.

Being born in the City of Sin, as all of us are, it is as though we are born in prison. And a prisoner who is born thus, who has never been outside its walls and has never heard stories of liberty, knows nothing of the natural freedom beyond the unnatural prison. But again, I am implying that *I* have escaped and know what lies beyond the horizon. So the question remains, "If you and I are born evil, how can we know what is good?"

For example, one asks, "Is adultery wrong?"

"Yes."

"Are you sure? What if it provides happiness and enjoyment? What about stealing? Is theft wrong?"

"It is."

"How do you know? What if I only redistribute money from the wealthiest in the world who *obviously* don't need billions anyway? Or what if I'm harmlessly watching a free movie link? What makes these things bad?" (Notice how a plethora of excuses escorts each evil act in an attempt to justify the deed.)

God observed this predicament and, in gracious mercy, provided proofs of our sinful nature.

Firstly, whether learned or simple, rich or poor, or technological or primitive, our hearts have all been endowed with a natural law. As the Founding Fathers so precisely put it, this natural law is "self-evident." It shouts, "This is the way!" when promoting an action or thing that is good, and it is at peace when an action is upright. In the same way, the conscience pleads when evil is about to be committed, "Stop! Don't do this!" And it mourns when sin is present.

Indeed, the common man cheers and rejoices when a serial killer is apprehended and forced to endure justice.

From the moment they possess the capacity to do so, man explores walking the line of this morality through the mechanism of conscious volition and application. Some enjoy flirting with the edge of the line, thus earning a reputation as a rebel in the making, and some downright cross the line, rendering to themselves the designation of "criminal." An astute child investigates the parent's tolerance for enforcing their communicated law by inching ever closer to its limit but never over it. If the child does step over that line, the law of the home is violated, and punishment is rightfully administered. As it is with all things, some children possess a proclivity to stay near the line and continuously "push our buttons" while others prefer to stay far away from it.

Or, for other examples, an apathetic employee works as little as possible before the boss discovers such laziness, and the unrepentant addict purposefully

The Law

wanders to see just how close to the vice he can get before temptation overcomes him and he capitulates to worldly desires.

The longer man experiments with these lines, the more the separation between good and evil becomes distorted. The natural law cannot be mocked. Think of this law as a lieutenant relaying battle orders from the admiral's destroyer to the troops storming a beach in the middle of an invasion. All is well and understood before the first bullet flies, but no one can anticipate the horrors of war and the confusion a battle creates. If the soldiers disobey the lieutenant's orders, they sabotage themselves into chaos and draw ever nearer to annihilation by the organized enemy. With each disobedient misstep the soldiers commit, intentional or otherwise, the lieutenant is forced to bark louder and louder in an attempt to regain control and reorganize his troops. Eventually, the sound of the lieutenant's frantic voice is drowned out by the enemy's guns, bombs, tanks, and reinforcements. Their platoon's fate is utter destruction on the beachhead.

The law of nature operates in the same capacity and will be silenced if we ignore it long enough. And not only will it be silenced, but it will later be reconfigured and allowed to speak again as a perverted compass. What is good will be called evil. What is evil will be called good.

We, even as sinners, understand the concept of the moral law. Returning to the City of Sin after a campaign, the gentle, yet firm, voice of the Christian's Commander cannot be cleared from the conscience. Day and night whispers of Christ, "Prisoner! Turn around and recognize what is beyond the opaque gates by which you are bound!" Although we serve the Empire of Self, God still cares for us and has implanted in each person a moral compass so that we might conclude amidst the tyranny of sin that "Something isn't right. Something is wrong."

But be careful. The longer one neglects to listen to moral convictions, the closer the conscience becomes like a trumpet in a towel—making noise, but no one can hear it.

But if we are evil, is this idea of a conscience and natural law not a contradiction? Didn't we choose to rebel against God? Why then would we feel vile and wicked after committing sinful acts? Have I not told you that our prideful spirit and flesh exist in continual opposition to God's law and is elated when we engage in evil?

O but the contrary is true! The torment of shame that one endures after committing wrong serves only to affirm that God has placed a moral conscience in our hearts. But because of the common case of the moral law within the individual becoming so confused that it puts evil for good,[4] God mercifully provides another guide.

---

[4] Isaiah 5:20

This evidence of our fallen nature is also proved through written Law. Not *a* law, but *the* Law. The Ten Commandments, as you and I commonly recognize them, are part of that Law, which, in total, contains 613 laws. It is deceptively comforting to assume that this Law was written to provide a list of rules and regulations that describe the series of physical attributes we must abide by to obtain righteousness and avoid punishment. That is to say: we believe the Law is the guide that reveals the process for obtaining perfection through works. From what I have seen and heard, this concept is what the majority of humanity understands the purpose of the Law to be.

Many, therefore, believe that the concept of morality must be an outward and physical phenomenon because that is what the Law appears to describe. I too seized this worldview with an iron grip, and it wasn't until after an embarrassingly long period of sin that I realized I was dead wrong (literally!). "Outwardly," I thought to myself, "I *must* uphold the Ten Commandments, because if I don't, I'll forfeit any gain I have made toward holiness and receive rightful condemnation to Hell as my punishment." I now understand that I was wrong.

Everyone who has been conceived, from the moment of their conception, has been or still is, a citizen of the City of Sin. You are no exception to this reality, and neither am I. Just as a person born in Canada is Canadian and a citizen of Russia is Russian, we are therefore, as members of this city, properly branded under our rightful designation as "sinners." After all, a citizen swears an oath, implicitly through their parents or explicitly themselves, to abide by the rules and ethics of their country and to defend that country if needed. In your case and mine, our parents pledged their allegiance to sin. Being their heirs, we have thus inherited their dead nature of sin, though we did not ask for it.

But there exists something beyond this City of Death—something new, something better. Yet the fortification of our pride is constructed high enough around the city that no resident can see beyond its gates, and the spiritual battlefield takes place in a wasteland with no visible landscape on the horizon to contradict our worldview.

If this were the conclusion of the story, if we could never see what is perfect, that should be the end of the matter. Your assertion that "we do not know what is objectively wrong" is correct and there would be no transgression against God, because there would be nothing absolute to transgress. Though the natural law would continue to exist, men would undoubtedly argue that it too was a social construct and is thus subjective and non-binding. Each act, whether one likes the act or not, is reduced to individual preference and opinion. There might be a constructed law of men, but it would merely be the current ideals of the ruling party...But that is not the end of the story.

Though we are naturally steeped in transgression, Christ, working through His followers, distributes this Law to sinners throughout the City of Sin. For the Law is a spiritually golden, clearly divine document forged in the fire of eternity, gifted in a wilderness, and printed not by man, but by the Divine. It was first gifted to a people God set apart for Himself: the Israelites, by whom He would rescue the world from sin. God's intention was for the Israelites, now endowed with the law, to present the wonder of the Lord throughout the sinful world by obeying the commands of the Law in faith. The Law, containing a description of God's character, righteousness, justice, and mercy, was the standard that Israel would proclaim. The Christian, presently, engages in the same type of evangelism by first proclaiming the Law, letting men and women read, witness, and recognize their failure to uphold this standard of perfection before an infinite God, and then preaching salvation through Christ Jesus.

Let us now discuss the obscure statement: *Though we are naturally steeped in transgression, Christ, working through His followers, distributes this Law to sinners.* In fact, I hold no reservations in stating that this Law is even "gladly" proclaimed to our sinful race by the emperor, Satan himself.

"This makes no sense," you may counter. "If we are inherently evil, and this Law proves it to us by stating what is good, won't we know what is good and so stop doing evil? Why would our emperor, Satan, want us to have this Law?"

Ah, Satan wants us to have these commands because the Law gives us a perverse power—assuming that power is to bow ever lower to our sinful self, like an alcoholic exercising his power to have a drink and losing his sobriety. The power is allotted not to the "good" portion of the man, for there is no good portion, but aimed at the sinful portion. Upon viewing the righteous Law, the individual spirit of pride, not willing to bow down to anyone but himself, has been loaded with the ammunition necessary to ensure unwavering loyalty to sin.

This Law, in telling us what we cannot do, is actually telling us what we must do. The same is true for the opposite; the Law, telling us what we must do, is also telling us what we must not do. But be careful. A commonly preached, but misunderstood, doctrine goes thus: sin rejoices at the giving of the Law, because the Law tells us exactly what we need to do to be holy, so the Law tells us exactly what we need to do to be sinful. A 1968 Dodge Charger set up with a 426 Hemi and racing slicks can slowly cruise through a neighborhood, but it's not fulfilling what it was built for: that is, to race. Though not incorrect, the concept that the Law is purposed to tell us what we can and cannot do is to utilize it wrongly.

Instead of telling us exactly *what* we need to do to be holy, the Law tells us exactly *who* we need to become to

The Law

be holy. Therefore, the Law is telling us *who* we need to be to be sinful. The answer to the holy *"who"* is Christ. The sinful *"who"* is, of course, us. Our spirit and body will faithfully rise to the occasion and live in sin, just as Christ's spirit and body faithfully rise to live in holiness.

As for us, sin recognizes this as a glorious opportunity to further inflame our pride and bring about true transgression. In the first place, sin often and very successfully, I might add, tempts us into the arrogant assumption that *we* are the holy one who can fulfill the Law, even though all others who have tried never succeeded. Tempting us, the emperor goads man to "live by the Law." If we are like the Pharisees, we believe we are living perfectly even when our intolerable self-righteousness damns us to Hell. On the opposite end of the spectrum, some recognize, based on failure after failure, the impossibility of upholding the Law and collapse low into depression. However, perhaps such a state brings one closer to ascension.

Sin also realizes that, in telling us the attributes of the righteous one, the Law also tells us the attributes of the wicked one. Because we are naturally slaves to sin, we are forced to do what we do not want to do. Our proclivity is to engage in acts opposite of God. So, when the Law says, "You shall not lie," my patriotic spirit of self states, "I will lie!"

When the Law dictates, "You shall not covet," my spirit decides it will covet.

"You shall not commit adultery."
"I must go and commit adultery!"
And so on.

Furthermore, when the Law is understood, we realize it proclaims, "Prove you are equal to God; prove you are absolutely righteous by abiding by every rule perfectly."

In response, we are supposed to say, "I cannot!"
Instead, our pride thinks, "I can! Watch."
Wrong.

The mere attempt of the self trying to uphold the Law breaks the Law. But perhaps you have never uttered a lie, you have never been unjustly angry, you have never disrespected your parents, and you have never stolen or committed adultery. You are still as sinful as I am (which means you are *very* sinful) because righteousness is not rewarded for keeping the Law. This makes sense if we remember that sin is *not* the failure to do the physical things the Law says to do. Sin is not lying, cheating, and stealing. Granted, as proof that our attempt to be equal to God is vain and hopeless, it is true we cannot physically uphold the Law—a fact revealed *through* lying, cheating, stealing. But sin is simply the spirit of "I" or "I alone am enough." The more you attempt to uphold the Law on your own and under your own strength, the more your evil increases because you are engaging in such activity without God.

You argue, "Well God is being unfair! In fact, not only is He unfair (based on my proposed view of fairness), but He is also cruel—toying with us like a slaveowner dangling water in front of a parched slave. Why would He give us a Law we cannot keep?"

But you have just answered your own question. The purpose of the Law was never that we would keep it perfectly, but that we would realize that we cannot. The Law is not a list of rules and regulations but a *picture of a person* who will fulfill that Law. Perhaps He already has.

That is not to say we cannot do good things of value. Extending kindness through friendly conversation with your neighbor, helping an elder unpack groceries, refusing to join in evil actions with others, and enjoying company with family and friends are all very good things to do, and for that reason, we ought to do them. But doing those things brings us no closer to righteousness—any more than it does a math student arguing he deserves to receive an A+ in linear algebra because he submitted an essay in English class. Furthermore, if we accept the proposition that the Law describes someone, then attempting to attain righteousness by keeping the Law is akin to arguing the absurd proposition that, if we act like someone, we actually *become* that someone.

So, although this law introduces condemnation, God is not "cruel" in supplying it to us. On the contrary, it is an act of utmost mercy. Without the Law, the pride which I serve would continue to rock me asleep with the gentle lullaby of my supposed eternal security though my good works until it's too late and death tracked me down for its payment.

In fact, I remember clearly the typical scenario of my life after the conclusion of a day of fighting for the empire. I would stagger home to that City of Sin I used to love and find at my door a crisp, clean envelope, addressed to me with my name written in fine calligraphy. It was my paycheck for my service to the City of Sin. I had served my emperor faithfully and with distinction, so I expected a handsome compensation. I picked it up slowly, opened it carefully, and read it. My heart sank as I realized my wage was the same as it was time and time before: *death*. It ceased to matter that I received the check repeatedly. Whether I was paid 10,000 times or 10, I only had to cash one check to obtain my compensation. Sin is only needed for a moment to justify an eternity in Hell.

More than that, it didn't matter how much I did for my emperor or how diligently I completed his every wish. The paycheck was never a little more and never a little less than death. I am confident to say that normally, if a man is paid the same sum of compensation irrespective of how hard he works, he will work as little as possible. If a man is paid $100 for working as hard as he can 8 hours a day or is paid $100 for sitting on his phone doing nothing, we expect him to do nothing. We logically expect this behavior because, in doing nothing, the man is actually earning more than $100. He is earning $100 plus the opportunity cost (his time—whatever its value might be) that used to be devoted to hard work. But sin does not obey the laws of classical economics. Though my wage was the same with each successive check, I worked harder and harder in rebellion against God.

Each time I received a new envelope, I would hope and wonder that it might be some sort of other compensation. A paycheck of money would have been welcome. I could've used that neutral method of exchange to purchase material goods and hopefully find happiness and satisfaction in the pleasure of utilizing those things. Maybe my pay would include power, fame, joy, or peace (peace would have been a wonderful trade), but it never arrived. I realized that what I really wished for was freedom from slavery to Satan's empire. I found myself consistently existing in a state of flux. Either my intellect and my will were perfectly aligned, craving evil and proving my slavery, or what my intellect desired and what my will wanted were two completely different things, again restraining my freedom.

Of course, none of us have kept the Law to the perfection God requires. If you really believe you have, you are making the very bold truth-claim that *you are God* or that you're equal to God. I do not suppose I should believe such a statement any more than you should believe me if I told you that *I* was God. I have no evidence to prove my claim, and neither do you. We cannot give sight to the blind with a word. We cannot calm the waves of the oceans. We cannot raise the dead. And we cannot forgive the sins of those who have not transgressed against us. But there is a man who can.

Tremble, therefore, before the righteous requirement of the Law and your failure to uphold it. See that you cannot measure up against Christ. Recognize your need for Him alone as Savior before it's too late! The Judge must try all in His court, and our trial, and the evidence compiled against us, is being prepared as we speak.

V

The Necessary Qualification

Of course, wholly believing the Son to be the sole justifier of individual man requires absolute submission, and that is nothing short of a description of Hell for the pride.

But we are getting ahead of ourselves. We have discussed it implicitly already, but we must now dissect the term "justification" and comment on what it means. Thankfully, scripture has whacked us over the head, repeatedly, with the reality that we are separated from God because of our sin. I have, and will continue to do, the same in this book. As has been said before, sin is to be void of His presence; where sin is, God cannot be. By definition, sin is the absence of God. To argue that the Divine can coexist alongside sin would be to argue that a circle is square.

Our flesh engages in many schemes to achieve salvation on its own. We have scratched the surface of trying to live by the Law as a tempting option for desired purification, but it is evident that it does nothing to bring God within us. The All-Seeing observes every last detail and flaw regarding our persons, our nature, our actions, and our hearts. Surely, it is impossible to gain righteousness by upholding the Law. If God's promise to redeem the sinner who desires reconciliation is to be upheld, another solution must be available. Someway, somehow, if I am to be with God in companionship and relationship, I must *justify* my reason for being allowed to be with Him. That is *justification*—the legitimization of our claim of living in Heaven on Earth with the Divine Trinity forever.

It is a fanatical suggestion—one the sinner, at judgment, shall learn is not rooted in truth—to suppose that they can approach the Infinite and demand, "I deserve to be with You because of who I am" or "I deserve to be with You because of what I have done." The Lord might even hear, "I deserve to be with You because of what I have done, making me who I am."

By utilizing any of these approaches of attempting to persuade God of our perceived perfection, we immediately prove ourselves to be hypocrites, for all three statements implicitly imply the absence of God and absolute sovereignty within man. Or, can you imagine that thought of you and I, soldiers from the empire, crossing over to the enemy's line and declaring, "I will fight for you on your side," all the while continuing to pledge allegiance to the City of Sin? We refuse to take off the colors and armor of evil and yet expect to dine with Christ as a family member around His banquet table. It is a logically incoherent scenario and one that does not in any way justify us before God.

VI

The Married Bachelor – Part I

But perhaps it is nothing more than a trivial inconvenience that righteousness cannot be gained by the Law. Even if the sinful individual concedes the reality that perfection cannot be obtained through the Law, pride is quick to regroup, reposition, and regain the previously held tactical advantage. Pride states, "Do not fear. There are, no doubt, other ways to obtain the perfection you desire. Come now, the eternal scale of good and evil is nearby. Let's weigh ourselves, and I'll prove that your good works will vindicate you."

Before we stand on the scale, we must remember that the concept of "good" cannot be an arbitrary description of the state of the world as you subjectively like it. It is an infallible standard by which all of us are judged. For if I regard something as "good" simply because I like it, and you regard that something as "bad" or "evil" because you don't like it, neither one of us possesses the necessary requirements to determine the correctness of one's opinion over the others. More than that, if I regard something as good because I like it, and you regarding something else as good because you like it, we again, under a naturalist standard, fail to determine whose good is the superior of the two. If people are all there is, and if all persons are created equal in their intrinsic worth, I cannot assume that what you regard as good to be any less than what I regard as good. Similarly, you cannot state that what you value as good is any more valuable than what I value as good.

However, if it is true that some men are "created more-equal than others," as our post-modern contemporaries conclude, then a group *can* determine what is right and what is wrong. The ruling class of Big Brother determines what is right, good, and proper because it holds the capacity to do so. If the group is challenged on their interpretation of good and evil, the declared oppressors are barraged with cries of "Bigot! Racist! Sexist!" and labeled with every "phobe" conceivable. This inevitably leads to the destruction of society as friend turns against friend, neighbor turns against neighbor, and family turns against family due to differing ideas of what perfection entails.

Of course, in our everyday lives, we see that objective good and evil exist apart from the subjective dictation of a ruling party. Joseph Stalin's starving of millions of Ukrainians was evil, and the horror of concentration camps can be felt to this day. But a young family having a barbecue with their neighbors—the men relaxing, the children playing in the yard, the women chatting and laughing together, and everyone enjoying each other's company on a hot day—is good. The biblical ordination of marriage is good. Charity to the needy is good.

Indeed, many things are objectively good. Therefore, this introduces a necessary being transcendent from the box of good and evil that you and I live in. This Spirit, being the moral law-setter, is the absolute definition of what good is. In other words, He is the absolute standard by which the otherwise infinite regression of moral relativism ceases. The divine being is God. To act like God is to act good, and to act opposite of God is to commit evil—not just outwardly, but within the heart. For example, when we give money to a homeless man, this is good because it reflects the attributes of God, namely charity and provision. If, instead, we mock and insult the poor, this is evil because it does not reflect God and His qualities.

But let us not cease this analysis yet. If we give charity to a homeless man *without anyone knowing*, this is excellent because it demonstrates the attributes of God, namely kindness, compassion, love, humility, and sacrifice. If, however, we give charity to a homeless man *and let everyone know it* (whether on a vlog or on the street), we commit evil because our hearts do not reflect God and His attributes. Instead, we engage in the attributes of Satan: self-exaltation, arrogance, and the humiliation of the homeless man. When we live in sin with our spirit of "I," it is the apex of acting opposite of God because we declare that we do not need God. This summit of sin cumulates with the unforgivable blasphemy of the Holy Spirit. Such a rejection of the Spirit is unforgivable because the Spirit is required for God to forgive.

It appears this ought to be the end of the chapter. If we act like God, we do good. If not, we do evil. Therefore, many conclude, as so many religions preach, that if we act like God more often than not, our good works will outweigh our bad and we will be declared righteous. But partial righteousness is *complete* wickedness.

Suppose that one early morning, in an act of wickedness and tragedy, someone covered by the stillness of silent night murders your neighbor. After a painstakingly long investigation, the authorities apprehend the murderer and transport him to court. In this court, as it should be, murder is a very serious offence. If the suspect is proven guilty of the crime, it is punishable by death.

After listening to the testimony of both the defense and the prosecution, a recess of one week is declared so the presiding judge can contemplate the facts and formulate a decision. To the initial surprise and gradual anger of many, the defendant is released into society on bail for the week of recess. We properly shake our fist at such an allowance, and although this assumption may appear unrealistic, and more importantly, wrong, our actual beliefs on the matter are quite the opposite.

During this week of recess, the defendant postulates that it might be favorable to his outcome if he gets on the judge's good side. Perhaps, assuming he will be found guilty, he hopes to reduce his sentence to solitary confinement, or life in a regular prison, or to twenty years served. Or, if he made a well-enough impression, maybe his sentence could be vetoed entirely, and the judge and he could then become, if not friends, at least cordial acquaintances.

The very notion of this scenario existing even as a hypothetical should make us wretch violently and squirm in our seats due to the proposed perversion of law, but let us continue.

Every day during the recess, the accused walks to the judge's home and performs various chores and jobs in an attempt to appease him who holds his fate. The murderer mows the judge's lawn, cleans his house, washes his cars, does his dishes and laundry, buys his groceries, and among other things, also cooks the family meals. The killer is inviting and friendly with the judge and does his best to keep from making mistakes and messing up. From the defendant's perspective, he is clearly worthy of some sort of mercy because of all his hard work throughout the week.

At the conclusion of the recess, all members are gathered back into the court to hear the ruling. With his judgement, the judge sentences the murderer to death. Members of the court rightfully praise and jump for joy at the legitimate exercise of proper judgement, but the defendant proclaims a different sentiment.

"What?! How could you? I did so much for you over the course of this last week. How could you not afford me at least some kind of mercy?"

You and I see right through this attempt at disfiguring justice, and so does the judge. The works of the criminal during the recess were parallel with the character of goodness, true, but what value do such works possess in acquitting the defendant of his wickedness committed beforehand? You are not squared from previous debts by promising to pay all subsequent loans. A man's life for a week's worth of work is not an adequate trade—all the more so when we realize individual life is inherently endowed with infinite value.

But what about a life for a life? Is giving up your life, because you took someone else's life, a legitimate trade? As a matter of fact, it is—provided the exercise of justice is sentenced by a judge and not a vigilante. The Lord Himself declares that a life for life,[5] pronounced by a judge, is the just punishment for murder. Quite simply, God is saying, "If you take a life that is not yours to take, then your life must be taken also."

---

[5] Deuteronomy 19:21

But do not be misled. That does not mean that you can save a life to repay your murder. Suppose the murderer saved the judge's life at some point throughout the week. Would the murder's judgment be forgotten? By no means, but why? Suppose two children, Pax and Irae, are playing in a sandbox at school. Further suppose that Irae, for no apparent reason, decides to hit Pax. After this altercation, Irae sees two other children fighting; he rushes over and breaks up the fight. Does Irae's peacemaking cancel out his original sin of hitting Pax? We should hope not! Irae's sin is against Pax and cannot be repaid by helping others.

This is why all our "righteous acts" are compared with filthy rags. The physical works we engage in may appear righteous, but in light of our crimes that have been committed, they are useless, dirty, and fit for the fire. The works have no power in cleansing a sin that has already corrupted the spiritual nature. The wage of sin is death, so nothing but death can satisfy the Law.

Furthermore, ask yourself: was the convicted murderer doing these "good works" out of the goodness of his own heart?

It is a laughable proposition. On the contrary, the works were enacted because of a false hope of the preservation of his individual being, not to serve the judge joyfully. In fact, if the criminal had never broken the law, it is dubious that he would have ever cared for the judge at all.

But what if an argument presents itself that states: What if the murderer believed he was doing the right thing? What if he sincerely believed the murder was formulated out of the goodness of his own heart?

Before I answer, let us amend this question to encompass *all* sin. Instead of confining the argument to murder, let it say: What if the *sinner* believed he was doing the right thing? What if he sincerely believed the sin was out of the goodness of his own heart?

The problem with such an argument is that its foundation for objection is predicated on the false presupposition that a person can possess a genuine desire to do good while simultaneously knowing they are committing a sin. For the Law is good[6] and to sin is to transgress against the Law, thus transgressing against the good. If a person knows the law, if they know the commandment "Thou shall not murder,"[7] then the idea of murdering someone "out of the goodness of their own heart" becomes logically incoherent. For we know that no one is good except God alone,[8] and as such, any goodness present in an individual is God's qualities being made manifest. Because sin is the separation of God, when one commits sin, their heart *cannot*, by definition, be attempting to do good because they are attempting to separate themselves from God, who is the good.

---

[6] Romans 7:14-25
[7] Exodus 20:13
[8] Luke 18:19

True, most societies become so morally twisted and corrupt that what is evil looks good and what is good looks evil.[9] But such corruption does not negate the absoluteness of the Law. What God declares as good, is good, even if subjective man perverts it. It is also true that our hearts have the devious proclivity to promise us that the righteous ends justify the sinful means. Of course, if we utilize sinful means to obtain righteous ends, then the ends themselves becomes sinful.

But more than that, back to our story of the murderer, what if, while engaging in the week of works, the accused consistently emphasized his hatred for the rest of the judge's family—perhaps through the usage of explicit statements like "I detest your children," or perhaps it is a refusal to acknowledge that the rest of his family even exists—then I can clearly hear the judge's rebuttal at the convict's outburst upon hearing his judgment: "You believe these works were for my benefit? Oh, on the contrary. Were they not for yours alone? Firstly, your works have no relation to your past act of evil. Secondly, the entire time you were with me, I heard you accusing and degrading my family. I witnessed your cruelty and dismissive indifference to those who love me and call me their father. After all, actions speak louder than words, and your words were already sufficiently loud. I see your manipulation, and I see your deceit. I am not mocked, but you have attempted to mock me by

---

[9] Isaiah 5:20

pulling the wool over my eyes with your sly pride. Your 'good works' became a slap in the face because of the genuine enmity that resided in your heart against me."

If there remains any doubt, I might admit that our example describes an impossible reality. We programmed the scenario to exist in a dimension where the accused was allowed to roam free during the week of recess so we could adequately express the metaphor. In reality, during the "week of recess," we remain in the city of spiritual sin from which we came—the city where the walls are infinitely high, where good is put for evil and evil for good and where God is separated from humanity.

Of course, you and I are the murderers and God is the Judge. Not only did we declare our hatred for His Son, we killed Him. I do not believe I need to articulate further.

VII

The Married Bachelor – Part II

From my temporal eye, I observe my good works arranged on the spread of life, adorned for others to see and praise, at the banquet of the worldly celebrating my visible accomplishments. All admire and gawk at the brightness of the golden glow emitted by the works according to their publicity.

"See how I have never stolen a thing? Look here, I have never committed murder. Oh, and don't forget that time I donated $1,000 to the church. And not only did I do good things and not do bad things, but I also had much success. See here? I was promoted to manager at 24, vice president at 30, president at 38, and CEO at 45."

The patrons applaud and congratulate on a life well-lived. But there is another attendee at this banquet: the judge, and he sees a much different display—a much more truthful one. My good works are revealed to be little more than garbage. Their nature is fit only for the Sanctum of Satan and the eventual House of Hell. The world celebrates these accomplishments I champion and exclaim, and thinks to itself, "Now there is a successful, righteous, citizen, that all ought to emulate." But God sees a fallen, broken man. In the eyes of the Divine, my works shine little more than dirt. The Lord does not desire them any more than a parent wishes their child to walk in the house and present them with a mud-pie gift on their clean carpet. Irrespective of the child's intention, the "present" is unwanted.

That is not to suppose that God does not desire to see people reflect His nature and do good. Not at all! What it does suppose is that, without faith in God, the concept of good works is worthless. Faith in Christ is what makes the work "good." Faith is what turns a mud-pie on the carpet into an apple pie on the counter.

Therefore, recognize the futility of attempting to sacrifice our good works as an offering to God for the atonement of our infinite transgression. Because God Himself *is* the good, then without Him, works considered perfect under the righteous scale are facades, like trying to paint a wall without paint. To step up and weigh ourselves on the scale of good works versus bad is to lose already. We step on the balance opposite of Christ, opposite of good, on evil. We are not measuring our excess of good, but how bad we are compared to how good Christ is.

Our attempts of reconciliation with God through works is akin to trying to pick up a bucket while you stand in it. If righteousness could be gained through the Law, why would Christ, who is God, allow Himself to suffer and die on a cross?[10]

When Christ announces, "I am the door,"[11] the Christian understands it to mean that Christ is the only way into the house of the Father in Heaven. But many believe this metaphysical door is still hidden above the clouds atop the mountain of Sinai where the Law was given. The individuals who desire to scale this mountain of the Law with each good work they do have hope that they can reach the summit and attain eternal life. They forget that all those who touched Sinai at the giving of the Law died.

If I am an unbeliever, I am a natural—although pre-fall of man unnatural—being of absolute bad. I know this because I am subject to death, both spiritual and physical, under the judgment of perfect Law. Even if I want to do good my good works are wicked, for I am a being of evil. I am a being of bad because, along with the definitions we have already discussed, we can define good as how closely a being conforms to its intended nature. If the pencil does not write, it is bad. If the lamp gives adequate light, it is good. Man's intended nature is to serve God absolutely, and that is good. The nature of our

---

[10] Galatians 2:20-21
[11] John 10:9

pride is to serve the self absolutely and is bad, being a deviation of the intended purpose of humanity.

More than that, being oppressed, my will and intellect are not unified, which is a constraint on my freedom. So, even if I in my mind want to do good, I cannot carry it out because my body wants to do bad. But, if I became a being of good, as the Law prophesizes, not by works, but by having the living good living in me, my works would be good. Similarly, when a work is not done in faith, it is sin, because sin consists of Christ *not* living in man.

There is another banquet that is commencing just down the street for a nobody. Although he has done his best to decorate the hall, it is in a grungy location that is dirty, dangerous, and poorly lit. No one, not even his family, has attended this, apparently very pitiful, celebration of life. There is nothing for him to put on his table spread, because all that he possesses is not of this world. His poverty of spirit, meekness, righteousness, persecutions, and all these things cannot be displayed with certificates, trophies, or money lest it invalidate all credibility. But then one patron arrives and right on time. It is the same judge from before, but this time, he is smiling and heaping congratulations of adoration and praise. What do we suppose he sees in this man the world deemed pathetic?

Our trial was already completed at our conception, and the charge was guilty. But there is a just solution. So,

I ask you, solider of Satan's empire, who would you rather be? A man despised by the world yet adored by God or accepted by men and rejected by the King? The battle is vicious, and your current emperor hates the Almighty. But this is the Gospel: that by placing your faith in Christ Jesus, the Son of God who died for your sins and was raised to life forever for your justification, you will become perfectly righteous.

VIII

The Temporary Reprieve

At the conclusion of your failed works argument, the Almighty declares, "No! Works cannot justify your desire for salvation. Only My Son can."

You respond, "Is there really no other way of justification at all?"

"None."

I mentioned before that the scripture states that the wage of sin to be death. The spiritual death is instantaneous at the moment of conception; the physical occurs sometime later in the future. By definition, a wage is not a gift; it is a lawful obligation. The employer is rightfully required to compensate the employee's sale of personal time, labor, and skills with the agreed wage lest the employer be appropriately taken to court for fraudulent behavior. So too, death is not credited to you and me "for the fun of it" or because the one who dictates the longevity of our temporal life is cruel. No, death is a reality of our lives because we are entitled to it as our wage for sin…but why?

God, being defined as the simplest standard of all morality, is by necessity perfectly just. If He was not perfectly just, we could assume a standard higher than Himself who judges His justice. If this is true, it turns the one we worship as God into merely a god.

Therefore, the Law, possessing the description of the attributes of God, is also perfectly just. Through our violation of the Law (which is really the abuse of God's person), we do not possess the perfect qualities of God and are thus unjust. If, in sin, we are not perfectly just, then the party who is perfectly just, being trespassed against through our injustice, must exercise the perfectly just judgement against us. If judgement is not enacted, then the Law is not just, because justice requires action, and it becomes nothing more than a list of empty words.

If the judgement is not *perfectly* just, then our sentence of death is perhaps unjust and warrants rebellion.

In order to satisfy the righteous requirement of the Law, the judgement for banishing God, who is life, from within oneself *must* be death. If death were not credited to us, God would not be perfectly just. Though you may be a god in your own eyes, you are not the God of life itself. How can you escape death if you harbor no sovereignty over it and what it does? What (or who) will give us the right and the confidence to stand before the Alpha and

The Temporary Reprieve

Omega and declare, very boldly I might add, "I deserve to have life forever in the full because…"

Let us return to our example of the murderer in the previous chapter. For the moment, suppose you are the criminal. You have just been sentenced to death for your crime and your head hangs low in hopelessness. Simultaneous with the drop of the gavel proclaiming the verdict's absoluteness, an unknown bystander stands up in the courtroom. He is rather young and normal looking. In a humble, quiet voice, he explains to the judge his desire, in the act of the highest mercy, to take your place in the den of death. This "nobody" has elected to do so because he desires that you might have life. He recognizes both aspects of the Law, the physical and the metaphysical, and wishes to temporarily save you from the physical. It is clear that both elements of justice cannot be administered through the actions of this unnamed man. He is merely extending your material life. In fact, justice is not produced at all. Only the physical, outward death, may be allocated to him.

After a period of brief deliberation, the judge concludes that this man is allowed to take your place. All parties recognize that this is not closure of any sort; it merely buys you a little more time. The guards lock your substitute in handcuffs and lead him away where he shall never be seen again while you stand there, free of restraints, in astonishment at what has just occurred. For the moment, the judge has begrudgingly accepted the substitution, but it is most certainly not a pardon for your crime. Death will still come to collect its bounty of your life, just not right then. Although absolutely selfless, this substitution has failed to abolish your sin, for you are still designated as the murderer. The outward and physical aspect of the punishment has been temporarily allocated, but that's all. There is a body in the grave, even though it's not yours.

What I have tried to describe is a picture of the Old Testament sacrificial system. Expressed in its most simplistic form, it is the killing of an animal in place of the individual as a temporary substitute for the penalty of sin, which is death. We shall discuss this later, but I mention this prematurely here because I wanted to note that, as I was writing the previous example, I was struck with confusion and began to question the validity of such sacrifice.

I have told you that the one true God who Christians worship is a God of justice, but this idea of substitution appears to be no justice at all. Of course, these questions arose from my own inadequate understanding of the sacrificial system, but after contemplation of the scriptures, it became clear. Does substitution of this nature satisfy the entirety of the perfect requirement of the Law? Not at all! Nothing about this system is just. Would the mother of a child, who had been tragically killed in a drunk driving accident, feel justice prevailed if an innocent bystander

The Temporary Reprieve

took the driver's place in prison? By no means, and that's the point! Such a substitute or sacrifice, if you prefer the term, is ineffective at cleansing sin and attaining righteousness. The answer to my problem is this: the ancient form of substitution was never intended for justice. In fact, it isn't any form of justice at all, and you and I intuitively know this.

It is so far from justice, and this certainly sounds counter-intuitive, that the substitute who takes your place in death is *not* receiving punishment. Under a legitimate law, punishment can only be administered once to the offending party. If a child randomly hits his brother, the parent ought to punish the child who hit the other. If the parent punishes both children, the exercise of justice is not proper at all. Or, if the parent punishes the offending child first after the incident and then punishes him three days later in addition, the parent has done wrong by disciplining the child twice for an infringement committed only once.

Though he is executed in your place, the substitute possesses none of your guilt, shame, disgrace, and sin, because he has not committed the murder. He is merely taking your place *if you physically received the wages of sin, death*. The guilt, shame, disgrace, and sin belong to you and you alone. True, if, by a miracle, your sin could be transferred onto him, then he would be receiving punishment, but what sinful person could do such a thing?

Do not misunderstand me. I do not wish to imply that the substitute is dodging the act of punishment; he is most certainly receiving your wage. The casket makes sufficient proof of that. Yet, while he has died, he himself has committed no crime and cannot, therefore, be punished under just law. If a parent disciplines a child having no evidence of any trespass against the law of the home, then it is not discipline at all. We rightly declare such actions to be abusive. To be punished without establishing guilt is tyranny, and God is not a tyrant.

Suppose we lived in a time before the first coming of Christ Jesus some 2,000 years ago. If we walk in sin, which we do, we walk with death. By definition, God, who is perfect life, cannot be amongst sin and death. Therefore, He can no longer naturally dwell among us (remember this is before Christ). Being sinners, under the just punishment of the Law, we deserve to be forever delivered over to death. Not only so, but the Father is justified in ending our lives the moment sin begins. Nothing was restricting His ability to strike down Adam and Eve the instant they ate the fruit.

"Wait!" says the Lord. "You who deserve to die immediately, sacrifice an animal in your place. This is to be your temporary substitute."

In our place, before the death of Christ, a substitute was offered in order to "cover" our sin from the eyes of God. This sacrificial animal could be a lamb, goat, bull, and so on, but it needed to be perfect. The high priest of the Jewish nation would take his hand and place it on the sacrificial animal. In doing so, he symbolically "transferred" over the sins of the individuals in Israel onto the animal. Let's use a goat for this explanation. The goat, and I am vastly oversimplifying, was then killed and drained of its blood—for the blood is the life of the animal—and the sacrifice was, for the sake of simplicity, complete. Through the sacrifice, the animal acted as a substitute and took the physical form of punishment that humanity was supposed to receive. It was as though we were on the altar. But an animal is not made in the image of God, and it has no power over sin and death itself, so it never possessed any capacity to eliminate sin entirely. Because animals cannot take away the sin of man, our sin was only momentarily "covered up" and "hidden" from the eyes of the living God.

Think of it this way. Suppose that sin manifests itself as a wound on your body, such as a cut. Further, suppose that, in order to be accepted in the presence of the perfect Almighty God, we must be free of all bodily wounds. This method of substitution animal sacrifice is like a band-aid. It covers the cut, but it does not remove the injury; it covers the actual sin, but it does not remove it. And, like cuts, sin is known to scar. The omniscient God "cannot see" the infirmity for the time being, but the contusion is still present and must not only be healed entirely, but be remade, in order to truly live perfectly and without fear of death.

If our blemishes of rebellion were to be covered, the unfortunate animal that was chosen to be subject to sacrifice needed to be perfect. No imperfections or defects were to be admitted—how can something that is broken hide what is also broken? How can a band-aid, cut in half and torn to pieces, cover a cut? An imperfect sacrifice would not—could never—be accepted by a Holy God. All the more so when we realize that the animal sacrifices of old were to be pictures of the Lord Jesus.

You may wonder why then was this solution only to be temporary? If the blood of a perfect animal can cover sin, why not just continue them *ad infinitum?* You might as well state to a person who has a chronic obstruction of airflow to their lungs (COPD), "You are suffering from COPD, but you live with an oxygen tank increasing your breathing capability. What's the problem?"

Of course, the answer is clear. Irrespective of the addition of forced oxygen, the COPD is ravaging the body of the sick. The disease has not been cured at all. Instead, the oxygen provides a muddy reality of what living without COPD might look and feel like, that is, breathing normally. Similarly, the sacrifices of old cured nothing regarding our sickness of sin. The proof of such sacrifice's failure to cure is found within the initial statement: if the blood of a perfect animal can cover sin, why not just continue them *ad infinitum?* Such sacrifices were never promised to cure, only cover.

The sacrifice needed to be performed repeatedly, because it could never complete the task of making filthy hearts pure, just as an oxygen tank for a COPD patient must be refilled.

I believe the book of Hebrews simplifies the matter very clearly when it states, "The sacrificial system was a shadow of the good things [Christ] that were coming. Not the reality them[Him]selves."[12]

When you observe your shadow on a bright sunny day, you recognize an absence, that is, the absence of light. Being very astute observers, you and I know that a shadow is an outline cast by a real, opaque object. So a shadow of yourself is not yourself but an absence of your physical self. The shadow is a description of your three-dimensional nature. You are required to fulfill the picture cast by the shadow, and without you, there is no shadow at all.

As we study the sacrificial system of old and its implementation within the law, we are really seeing the absence of the person who is required to fulfill the definition of perfection prophesied by the shadow: Christ.

More than that, we do not need to search extensively for scripture that reminds us that God was not at all pleased with the old sacrifices. What mother is satisfied with a doctor who, upon receiving her child who requires stitches, sends him home with a band-aid? The bleeding may have slowed, but the child is not cured. Or

---

[12] Hebrews 10:1

suppose your truck leaks from the gas tank. If the mechanic takes a piece of duct tape, covers the hole, and sends you on your way, will you be satisfied with your service? God may have been able to dwell near man under the old sacrificial system, but He could never dwell within him as He intended because the sin remained. Though we were outwardly clean through animal sacrifices, our hearts remained wicked and foul.

"Then there is no justice with this system at all!" you answer.

You're right, there isn't.

Enter Christ.

IX

The Solution for the Enigma of Life

As I sit in contemplation pondering how to describe my Savior and yours, I find myself in the extraordinarily difficult position of attempting to adequately explain a being simultaneously inhabiting a state of perfect individuality while exhibiting definitive duality (being both fully God and fully man simultaneously) in accordance with harmoniously existing eternally within the Divine Trinity. Because of this mammoth reality, which no mortal can understand in the land of the temporal, I have no trouble at all reconciling the statement that it will take an eternity to properly know and understand the fullness of Jesus Christ.

What I know of Him now and, by extension, what I know of myself is like a man looking at a friend through a dirty window. Although I cannot presently see him as clearly as I wish to, a consequence of my sinful body, I know that he exists and what his properties are. Soon the window, not only will be made clear, but it will be eradicated as I see him face to face.

So it is not surprising to you when I admit that all of my prior attempts to produce descriptions regarding Christ's nature have led to undesirable manuscripts, which have rightfully found their place at the bottom of the trash. They were not unfit for this book because they were too simple a description of Christ. On the contrary, they were not simple enough. When we talk about the qualities of our friend to another, we refrain from describing them with a long, drawn-out, more-intellectual-than-thou approach. An abstract philosophical metaphor detailing our friend is generally ineffective if others are to know who he really is. True, I do not discount the importance of discussing the metaphysical nature of Christ. Indeed, I have much interest and find much joy in researching and studying the topic myself, but I am commanded to proclaim the gospel as simply as possible. Similarly, I am not saying that metaphor and vivid imagery are unimportant or unwanted—we have used many in this book. But we talk about those we love in simple terms that are *true* so that that their personality and physical attributes might be recounted as clearly as possible.

For example, I could describe my earthly father to you in this way: He was not before 1959 and then he was. He hailed from that distant landscape foreign to the one I now inhabit as home. His early life all through his teen years was filled with countless hours of the backbreaking work under various weather conditions providing sustenance for others. After his childhood, he ventured to the nexus of his province to study the abstract, yet necessary, language of the universe. And so on. Based on this description, you know very little of him.

On the contrary, I should change my approach and describe my earthy father like this: Dad was born in 1959 in Springside, Saskatchewan. He grew up as a grain farmer with his family. When he was 18, he went to school in Saskatoon to study math and become a calculus teacher. And so on. My second description, utilizing simple and absolute descriptions, has produced a much more accurate representation than the first.

My Christ is not a Savior hidden under countless hours of intense philosophical, psychological, metaphorical, and metaphysical analysis. No, He is a *real*, physical person presented to us that we might know God. Yet our arrogance has convinced us that unless we contemplate Jesus and His teachings until we have arrived at an understanding profound and ethereal, then we cannot know Him as He really is. Christ's beatitudes do away with such a hypothesis. As a result, our children recognize, believe in, and know Him and who He is better than we adults, who are so wise and enlightened in our own estimation, do. The farmer, the homemaker, and the garbage truck driver, often have a far deeper, more intimate, and greater knowledge and faith in Jesus than the biblical professor, the psychologist, and the pastor, even with all their hours of study, translation, and teaching.

My last resort, and most certainly the approach I should have begun with, is to follow the direction of the apostles and simply describe Christ as I witnessed and now know Him to be.

If one is serious about knowing Christ as He really is, there is no better place to investigate His entire being than the scriptures. The gospels are excellent, and I believe it is vital to always be reading at least one out of the four, but I mean studying the whole scripture—Genesis to Revelation. In fact, I firmly argue the Old Testament stories provide some of the clearest pictures of Christ imaginable. Through the human, Adam, the Fatherhood of mankind is presented. Through Christ, not only is the Creator of physical mankind revealed, but "just as in Adam all die, so in Christ, all will be made alive."[13]

The story of Joseph, the favorite son of Jacob, articulates the overarching theme of Christ's life, death, and exaltation. That is to say, just as Joseph is initially exalted above all others, brought low into the pit of suffering because of the sinful actions by those he loves, and finally restored to a position of prominence and leadership throughout all the world, so too is Christ. Our Christ was the Lord over all creation, but our actions of

---

[13] 1 Corinthians 15:22

sin forced Him to be brought low to earth to suffer and die as punishment. But, because of His righteousness, God raised Him out of the pit, death, and has now glorified Him at His right hand.

As Moses rescues God's people who are slaves and then acts as mediator for Israel between them and God, so too Christ saves us from slavery to sin and is the one and only mediator between God and the individual. Though King David was a great king, in his physical descendant, Christ, I know a greater king is coming. Nehemiah wept for the Jews, and Christ not only wept, but died for them. Solomon had wisdom unparalleled, but that wisdom came from Christ. Joshua was a fearless warrior, but he only obtained that courage because Christ was with him. Boaz was generous and kind as is Jesus. Abel was martyred for his righteousness, and Christ was crucified. Elijah raised the dead; Christ is life…we can discuss these archetypes literally until the end of this age and we still would not deplete the literary resource of scripture.

Christ possesses a power that is unquantifiable, and yet He harnesses it to form the daisies in the field. In his left hand he holds the universe, some 93 billion lightyears in diameter, like a man holding a rubber ball. No comet from the Kuiper Belt travels farther than permitted, no planet spins faster than what it was designed, and no galaxy collides with another unless the Divine has appointed it so.

And in His right hand, Jesus takes care of me and personally fulfills my every need. He gladly graces me with his full attention. It is as though I am His one and only son. It's like I am the only man who has ever existed in the history of the world. Though I know Christ has many children, it is wonderful knowing I do not have to compete with them for His love.

All of the armies combined in the history of the world could not compare with the power of Christ, armed to the teeth with heavenly creatures, creatures so magnificent, intimidating, and ethereal that our greatest philosophical, scientific, and spiritual minds could never comprehend. Yet He ensures that those same angels will proclaim something so precious, tender, and innocent as birth.

The nature of God, personified through the being of Christ, is one I could—no, one I *will*—stare at for 1,000 years and never feel the slightest boredom. If we look at the face of a human, particularly of one we love, there exists an infinite number of infinitesimal changes in the countenance that produce new combinations and completely change their character. If you spend enough time with that person, you become aware of their acute expressions that no one else recognizes and they become yours alone to witness. How much more time will be needed for the One who gave us the ability to have expressions at all!?

It is inconsequential whether Christ's hair is long or short, whether He is 6'4 or 5'8, or whether His eyes are blue or brown. I love Him and wish to be with Him, not because of what He is, but because of *who* He is. Granted, the desire to be with my God is attainable because Jesus died on the cross. But a man loves his wife not because of what she accomplishes or what she does, but because she is *herself.* Let us not forget the opposite is true as well; a wife loves her husband not because he earns an impressive paycheck or because of his physique, but because he is himself. Christ dying on the cross is who He is—the sacrificial, suffering, subjected, Son of Man.

As a result of His subsequent resurrection and glorification, Christ alone is justifiable in condemning me, but He is also the only one justifiable in saving me, and that is what He does. His command of creation, the patriarchs, time, space, and life itself, prove to me that He was and is everlasting. Yet He was formed on this Earth with a mortal, physical body in order that I might know God. The being of Christ encapsulates every aspect of men we objectively deem admirable, praiseworthy, and true, and He amplifies them greater than anyone has ever known.

For this reason, I know that He alone is the rightful ruler of all humanity, despite subjugating Himself as a servant to those who would harm Him with suffering and death. I am the child of one who is forever a perfect harmony of both lion and lamb, in that He came and will come again to rule yet to serve, to punish yet to save, to be feared yet adored, to be slandered yet innocent, to reign yet to abdicate, to establish a heavenly kingdom yet be subjected to earthly empires, and to be majestic and brilliant yet to become like us but something much greater.

X

The Apex of Love

Far be it from me to retell the greatest story in the history of the world with my own words. What I have copied from Matthew 26:57-28:10 is not metaphor or myth, but wholly true. In fact, if you put this book down right now, never read it again, and instead read the crucifixion and resurrection of Jesus from the Bible itself, my purpose in writing this book is entirely fulfilled. I have nothing else to say on the subject, except to let the scripture speak and that upon this truth your eternal fate lies. This is the fulfillment of the person of Christ. My eternal and final substitute.

***

Those who had arrested Jesus took him to Caiaphas the high priest, where the teachers of the law and the elders had assembled. But Peter followed him at a distance, right up to the courtyard of the high priest. He entered and sat down with the guards to see the outcome. The chief priests and the whole Sanhedrin were looking for false evidence against Jesus so that they could put him to death. But they did not find any, though many false witnesses came forward.

Finally two came forward and declared, "This fellow said, 'I am able to destroy the temple of God and rebuild it in three days.'"

Then the high priest stood up and said to Jesus, "Are you not going to answer? What is this testimony that these men are bringing against you?" But Jesus remained silent.

The high priest said to him, "I charge you under oath by the living God: Tell us if you are the Messiah, the Son of God."

"You have said so," Jesus replied. "But I say to all of you: From now on you will see the Son of Man sitting at the right hand of the Mighty One and coming on the clouds of heaven."

Then the high priest tore his clothes and said, "He has spoken blasphemy! Why do we need any more witnesses? Look, now you have heard the blasphemy. What do you think?"

"He is worthy of death," they answered.

Then they spit in his face and struck him with their fists. Others slapped him and said, "Prophesy to us, Messiah. Who hit you?"

Meanwhile Jesus stood before the governor, and the governor asked him, "Are you the king of the Jews?"

"You have said so," Jesus replied.

When he was accused by the chief priests and the elders, he gave no answer. Then Pilate asked him, "Don't you hear the testimony they are bringing against you?" But Jesus made no reply, not even to a single charge—to the great amazement of the governor.

Now it was the governor's custom at the festival to release a prisoner chosen by the crowd. At that time they had a well-known prisoner whose name was Jesus Barabbas. So when the crowd had gathered, Pilate asked them, "Which one do you want me to release to you: Jesus Barabbas, or Jesus who is called the Messiah?" For he knew it was out of self-interest that they had handed Jesus over to him.

While Pilate was sitting on the judge's seat, his wife sent him this message: "Don't have anything to do with that innocent man, for I have suffered a great deal today in a dream because of him."

But the chief priests and the elders persuaded the crowd to ask for Barabbas and to have Jesus executed.

"Which of the two do you want me to release to you?" asked the governor.

"Barabbas," they answered.

"What shall I do, then, with Jesus who is called the Messiah?" Pilate asked.

They all answered, "Crucify him!"

"Why? What crime has he committed?" asked Pilate.

But they shouted all the louder, "Crucify him!"

When Pilate saw that he was getting nowhere, but that instead an uproar was starting, he took water and washed his hands in front of the crowd. "I am innocent of this man's blood," he said. "It is your responsibility!"

All the people answered, "His blood is on us and on our children!"

Then he released Barabbas to them. But he had Jesus flogged, and handed him over to be crucified.

Then the governor's soldiers took Jesus into the Praetorium and gathered the whole company of soldiers around him. They stripped him and put a scarlet robe on him, and then twisted together a crown of thorns and set it on his head. They put a staff in his right hand. Then they knelt in front of him and mocked him. "Hail, king of the Jews!" they said. They spit on him, and took the staff and struck him on the head again and again. After they had mocked him, they took off the robe and put his own clothes on him. Then they led him away to crucify him.

As they were going out, they met a man from Cyrene, named Simon, and they forced him to carry the cross. They came to a place called Golgotha (which means "the place of the skull"). There they offered Jesus wine to drink, mixed with gall; but after tasting it, he refused to drink it. When they had crucified him, they divided up his clothes by casting lots. And sitting down, they kept watch over him there. Above his head they placed the written charge against him: this is Jesus, the king of the Jews.

Two rebels were crucified with him, one on his right and one on his left. Those who passed by hurled insults at him, shaking their heads and saying, "You who are going to destroy the temple and build it in three days, save yourself! Come down from the cross, if you are the Son of God!" In the same way the chief priests, the teachers of the law and the elders mocked him. "He saved others," they said, "but he can't save himself! He's the king of Israel! Let him come down now from the cross, and we will believe in him. He trusts in God. Let God rescue him now if he wants him, for he said, 'I am the Son of God.'" In the same way the rebels who were crucified with him also heaped insults on him.

From noon until three in the afternoon darkness came over all the land. About three in the afternoon Jesus cried out in a loud voice, "Eli, Eli, lema sabachthani?" (which means "My God, my God, why have you forsaken me?")

When some of those standing there heard this, they said, "He's calling Elijah."

Immediately one of them ran and got a sponge. He filled it with wine vinegar, put it on a staff, and offered it to Jesus to drink. The rest said, "Now leave him alone. Let's see if Elijah comes to save him."

And when Jesus had cried out again in a loud voice, he gave up his spirit.

At that moment the curtain of the temple was torn in two from top to bottom. The earth shook, the rocks split and the tombs broke open. The bodies of many holy people who had died were raised to life. They came out of the tombs after Jesus' resurrection and went into the holy city and appeared to many people.

When the centurion and those with him who were guarding Jesus saw the earthquake and all that had happened, they were terrified, and exclaimed, "Surely he was the Son of God!"

Many women were there, watching from a distance. They had followed Jesus from Galilee to care for his needs. Among them were Mary Magdalene, Mary the mother of James and Joseph, and the mother of Zebedee's sons.

As evening approached, there came a rich man from Arimathea, named Joseph, who had himself become a disciple of Jesus. Going to Pilate, he asked for Jesus' body, and Pilate ordered that it be given to him. Joseph took the body, wrapped it in a clean linen cloth, and placed it in his own new tomb that he had cut out of the rock. He rolled a big stone in front of the entrance to the tomb and went away. Mary Magdalene and the other Mary were sitting there opposite the tomb.

The next day, the one after Preparation Day, the chief priests and the Pharisees went to Pilate. "Sir," they said, "we remember that while he was still alive that deceiver said, 'After three days I will rise again.' So give the order for the tomb to be made secure until the third day. Otherwise, his disciples may come and steal the body and tell the people that he has been raised from the dead. This last deception will be worse than the first."

"Take a guard," Pilate answered. "Go, make the tomb as secure as you know how." So they went and made the tomb secure by putting a seal on the stone and posting the guard.

After the Sabbath, at dawn on the first day of the week, Mary Magdalene and the other Mary went to look at the tomb.

There was a violent earthquake, for an angel of the Lord came down from heaven and, going to the tomb, rolled back the stone and sat on it. His appearance was like lightning, and his clothes were white as snow. The guards were so afraid of him that they shook and became like dead men.

The angel said to the women, "Do not be afraid, for I know that you are looking for Jesus, who was crucified. He is not here; he has risen, just as he said. Come and see the place where he lay. Then go quickly and tell his disciples: 'He has risen from the dead and is going ahead of you into Galilee. There you will see him.' Now I have told you."

So the women hurried away from the tomb, afraid yet filled with joy, and ran to tell his disciples. Suddenly Jesus met them. "Greetings," he said. They came to him, clasped his feet and worshiped him. Then Jesus said to them, "Do not be afraid. Go and tell my brothers to go to Galilee; there they will see me."[14]

---

[14] This entire story was quoted directly from Matthew 26:57-28:8.

XI

The Salvation of Man

It is deceptively simple to be snared in the trap of forcing some "profound" statement into a fundamental message that only unnecessarily complicates things and confuses the audience. In this case, such confusion may damn a man to Hell eternal. God forbid I should add to a message that is already perfect in its simplicity; I shall keep it short, and my analysis, brief.

Fundamentally, our entire discussion is constructed upon the metaphysical equation that Christ = Your Salvation. If God completely removes Himself from the world of man, then we cannot formulate this equation on our own. Mortal humanity, if we and creation are void of the Trinity, lack the necessary knowledge to even begin to contemplate such things. To say that we could uncover the mysteries of the Divine without any revelation from the Divine himself would be to argue that a detective can solve a crime he has never heard about. But through the general revelation of nature and natural law and the special revelation of scripture and His son, God has declared this magnificent equation to be the axiom of axioms. To add anything to this truth would be to declare that one plus maple tree equals two. It becomes incoherent.

But this profound claim that Christ is your salvation is true! Upon that rugged cross where He died, the punishment for your sin and mine was paid once for all eternity. Jesus' death is the final substitute in the sacrificial system. He is *the* sacrifice, *the* substitute. The person that cast the shadow of the ancient Law was finally revealed. Every line in the face, every tear from the eye, every smile from the spirit, every teaching from the mountain, and every prayer from the heart of Christ Jesus entirely fulfilled the description of God given to man.

Because He made Himself completely subject to the Father, demonstrating the heavenly hierarchy through His humanity, all that He was in eternity past (if I might be allowed to use "past" as a term when discussing uncreated things), all that He did on Earth, all that He is now in Heaven, and all that He is going to be in the future eternity is perfect and void of sin. For Christ never had the spirit of "my will alone" but of "your will, Father, alone." It is derivative of this righteousness, because He is God Himself, that Christ is declared to be the absolute offering for sin. It should have been me upon that cross, suffering unto death for my sin (and in one sense, it was), but instead, as Rembrandt painted so profoundly, I was positioned at the bottom, helping hoist my Lord, nailed to that cursed tree, high into the air.

Our continuing guilt, our hidden shame, our gnawing conscience, and our sin itself was placed on Jesus. By delegating the entirety of our sin to Himself, He became a void—void of life, void of comfort, and void of Heaven. Allotting our sin to Christ, logically, forced Him to be abandoned and in effect cut off from the Trinity. I do not dare attempt to comprehend the horror of what it must have been to experience eternity in Hell for a moment. The scream of anguish before His death arose from a fear that no man has ever yet known. Whips and beatings, mockery, ridicule, and embarrassment are horrible, but what are those compared to Him being the only eternal Son separated from his eternal Father?

Think of the wretched anguish of a loving mother whose infant child has just been kidnapped by an unknown figure under the shadow of darkness. Think of the helpless cry of a young husband or wife who has just learned their spouse has been killed in a car accident. Imagine the fear of hearing over the radio that a nuclear missile was due to detonate in your city within the next five minutes. Multiply these fears by an infinite amount to recognize our inability to understand the suffering that Christ endured at the cross.

We must articulate that the death of Christ does *not* provide immediate forgiveness for every person on Earth. We will not see every human who has ever existed in Heaven. It is for this reason we have been utilizing the terms "paid" and not "accepted." A charitable man might write a blank check and pay a desolate stranger's debts, but if the stranger never deposits the check and allocates the payment, the debt is not paid. The check might as well have never been written. In the same way, the invitation to receive absolute appropriation for sin is extended toward all, but if an individual rejects the salvation, then God shall honor the decision.

But as a Christian, it is a beautiful euphoria to know that my sin has been forgiven, yet it is inconsequential if Christ is still dead. Returning to the example of our stranger, suppose he cashes the check from the charitable man. The transaction is cleared with the bank, and the stranger is now a man free from crippling debt. That is all fine and well; in fact, it's excellent, but what if the stranger ends up receiving no benefits from clearing his debt? What if he pays his debt but has no way of earning a living? What if, even after removing all prior monetary obligations, he is forced to return to a homeless lifestyle? It might be that the bank refuses to treat the man any different than before because of his past credit history, but the result is the same. The stranger is relinquished back into poverty, and it is as though the check was worthless. The Christian, if Christ is still dead, might be forgiven of sin. But if the Christian's fate is the same as the wicked, then here is no absolute justice in this world or the world to come, and we cease to find purpose in Jesus. Indeed, "If only for this life we have hope in Christ Jesus, we are, of all people, most to be pitied."[15]

But Christ is not dead! He's alive! Literally, thank God, Jesus was raised from the grave! But for a moment, pretend that Christ stayed dead. Of course, if He is dead, He is no Christ and is only worthy of the title "Jesus." Suppose He was crucified on a cross, died, was laid in a tomb, and his bones lie there to this day…then I am a fool and my belief is fantasy. If Jesus is dead, then so am I. My continuing war against the Divine masquerades itself as "peace with God," my freedom in Jesus is slavery to sin, and my ignorance of the truth is strength for the emperor. The cumulation of my foolishness manifests itself through my hope of a resurrection sinking into the eternal grave.

On the contrary, the historical resurrection of Christ proves that our Father has accepted the sacrifice of His son. Therefore, sin has been paid, defeated, and annihilated once for all time. We might summarize our previous few thoughts with this generalization of the gospel: "Christ was delivered over to death for our sins, and was raised to life for our justification."[16] If we know

---

[15] 1 Corinthians 15:19
[16] Romans 4:25

The Salvation of Man

this to be true, then Christians ought to imitate Christ in all that they are.

Because He suffered, I will suffer. Because He forgives my sin, I will forgive others of sin. Because He has peace, I have peace. Because He has been raised from the dead, I will be raised from the dead. Because He lives eternally, I live eternally.

Think again of our friend, the stranger, and put him in a new situation. He has cashed the check from the charitable man. His debt is cleared. But in addition to this, the charitable man approaches the stranger and offers him a home, security, family, and a job to provide income. Not only have the stranger's debts been cleared, but he has been given a new name, a new identity, and a new hope in his "resurrected" life. He will never go into debt again for all past debts, and any future ones, have been taken care of. The stranger's old nature has been left behind and buried to make room for the new man.

But what if the new man refuses to work? What if he says to himself, "What's the use in working? All my past and future debts are paid so why not do whatever I want?" This is an excellent question, and one that will be answered later in the book. These questions of justification to sin versus justification *from* sin are discussed in the chapter titled, "The Gradual Liberation."

For the moment, let us focus on the fact that, in Christ, old nature, deserving of punishment, has been

— 97 —

crucified with Him. More than that, the new creation has been raised with Jesus—spiritually at the moment of repentance and physically shortly after.

Therefore, because of the wonder of the gospel and its transformative power, I am obligated by my Lord to ask you: Do you know Christ as your Savior?

If you are lost and lonely. If you are sick with sin and sorrow. If you long to be free from the slavery of Hell's empire. If you are exhausted with the futility of trying to find fulfillment in the world. If you recognize salvation does not originate within yourself. If you desire to be free from death and all fear of death. *Then* there is but one thing you must do—believe in your heart that Jesus is Lord. Confess with your mouth that He has saved you from your sin.

Is your soul parched from the journey of life? Are you crushed under the weight of sin? Will you turn to yourself, your co-worker, your spouse, or your government? What politician, speaker, intellectual, pastor, or family member has ever told you, "Come to me you who are weary and burdened, and I will give you rest"?[17] No. There is only one man who ever stated such a claim with absolute authority and legitimacy. Accept Christ as your Savior! He is the only path to eternal and everlasting life. It is by grace through faith that you and I are saved.[18]

---

[17] Matthew 11:28-30
[18] Ephesians 2:8-9

The Salvation of Man

Generally, when a person desires to be saved by Christ, we pray some variation of this "sinners prayer" with them:

"Lord, you are the God of Heaven and Earth. You are the Creator of all that exists. I know that You created man in Your image to be perfect. But I have sinned and rebelled against You, and I am deserving of death because of it. There is nothing that I can do on my own to be justified before You, a holy God. Yet You, in Your infinite mercy, sent Jesus Christ to die for my sin. Through His death on the cross, I know the punishment for my evil was paid. Three days later, Jesus rose again to live eternally and rule by your side proving Your acceptance of His sacrifice. I accept Christ Jesus as my Savior, and in Him alone, I place my faith. Cleanse me of my sin and make my spirit pure as Yours. Through Him, I am known to be perfect in Your eyes. Thank You, Lord, for my undeserved salvation. Thank You for Your everlasting love. Amen."

Usually, the Christian prays a sentence and then the desired convert repeats it back. Although there is nothing about such a method that voids the assurance of salvation, I find it to be clunky, awkward, and contrary to human nature. We are not robots programmed by creators to say things we do not mean. We are living, breathing organisms endowed with the beauty of spontaneity.

It is the fundamental doctrine of Christianity to reject the legalism that categorized the people that misinterpreted—and still misinterpret—the Law. As a product of this command, the decision about how to pray the prayer and in what order you say your words is of no consequence; what matters is your acceptance that Jesus is Lord.

To illustrate this point, suppose your young child ruins your living room carpet by disobeying your command not to trek mud into your house. When he or she apologizes, your concern is not with their ability to articulate cohesive, mature sentences that only adults can understand. The child's inability to formulate an eloquent speech describing their failure to uphold the law and their need for your forgiveness does not make their tearful "sorrys" any less acceptable. But we must be careful. Society has become so engulfed in looking only with their emotional eyes and not with their logical ones that any display of emotion determines a man's protest, proclamation, or plea to be truthful and correct. This view is lamentable and heavily contributes to the disintegration of societies. A lack of emotion in a child's apology does not make the attempt of reconciliation any less proper than the one who displays overwhelming emotion and tears. What you as the parent is concerned with is the condition of their heart.

Who is more righteous—the learned child with a cold logic who presents a thoughtful apology with the highest level of vocabulary they know yet holds enmity in his heart against you? Or the child who can only pronounce a broken, "I'm sorry for what I did," yet who genuinely desires forgiveness? In the same breath, we can ask the same question with the roles reversed. Who is more righteous—the learned child with a cold logic who presents a thoughtful apology with the highest level of vocabulary they know and has an earnest desire to see your relationship repaired? Or the emotional child who says, "I'm sorry for what I did," yet manipulates with tears to avoid punishment?

But God is never fooled. A man might make a grand public oration not only discussing but bragging about his sin and need for forgiveness. The witnesses clap and congratulate on a conscience well listened too, but God only recognizes a wicked spirit. On the contrary, the quiet husband might acknowledge his need for forgiveness, look up to the stars, and be near speechless as he chokes back tears and cries, "Have mercy on me, Lord. I'm a sinner and I need your salvation." There is nothing impressive about this type of prayer to the public eye, but in the heavenly court, such a man is said to have the poetic prowess of David.

Therefore, if you desire to utilize the sample prayer I have provided, do not be afraid about doing so. But I encourage you to ask for forgiveness from your heart. Let your prayer flow from your desire for life. Perhaps your prayer will be short: "Lord Jesus, cleanse my spirit from sin." Perhaps it will be an hour or two long. Those far more intellectual than I could ever hope to be might devise a prayer with diction I cannot understand or one might pray with words a four-year-old can string together. The result is the same: the forgiveness of sin and the guarantee of eternal life.

If you have made this commitment, you're saved! The moment you believed that prayer, at the very second you accepted Christ's salvation, the Holy Spirit descended into your heart (offering proof of your conversion), cleansed your spirit from acts and conscience that lead to death, and now lives within you eternally. All of your sins have been destroyed and disintegrated. But Christ has not left you with an empty chasm where your old rebellious nature used to reside. It has been replaced with something—no, *someone* new but still you. And this new being, you who have been reborn in the likeness of Jesus, is an eternal child of the Almighty God. Nothing you do or what anyone else does can ever take away your adoption to sonship in Christ Jesus. Sins, trials, temptations, sufferings, and death are all powerless in their desire to rip you from the hands of He who created the universe. Are you fearful you will sin too often in the future and Christ will rescind His salvation? Never forget, even in your most shameful sins, God is not constrained by time. Before the creation of the world, He knew the intricate details of your sin and mine. He knows exactly how many times each of us is going to sin and what the nature of that sin is. Despite all this, He has saved us still.

Christian, your sins of the past are paid, your sins of today are abolished, and your sins in the future are already forgotten by the Almighty God.

But before this chapter concludes, I should like to say one or two more things on a matter that afflicted me, especially in my younger spiritual years, and is perhaps causing a great deal of stress for you.

Perhaps there are some of you presently in the self-anointed lot of the "unforgivable sinner." Those who, when confronted with the promise of salvation, hang their head low in self-imposed shame and declare, "I cannot accept! Christ does not want me, for my sin is too great. You might think your sins were bad before you met Christ, but only because you have no idea what *I've* done. I am too sinful a person to be redeemed by Jesus."

Do not believe such a thing! It is a lie from the emperor. Rebuke Satan and have nothing to do with his rejection of truth.

But do you still have trouble believing? Remember the Apostle Paul. If Christ is the master-architect of Christianity, then Paul is his foreman. In his memoirs to his protégé, Paul discusses the circumstances regarding his conversion: "Christ Jesus came into the world to save sinners, of whom I am chief. But for that very reason I was shown mercy so that in me, the worst of sinners, Christ Jesus might display his immense patience as an example for those who would believe in him and receive eternal life."[19]

Paul is declared the worst of sinners, yet Christ's grace was awarded to Paul all the same. So it is with you, you who fear your sin is too vile to be forgotten, for there is no sin too great for Christ to overcome.

Similarly, one might contemplate, "I have accepted Christ as my Savior, but I don't feel any different. Am I saved?"

If you have believed in your heart that Jesus is your Savior, I guarantee that you are saved, because scripture guarantees that you are saved. Contrary to the apostasy committed by the popular church, our salvation does not rest on our emotions or feelings. The scriptures do not say, "We feel we will live eternally," but, "We *know* we will live eternally."

It is therefore nothing to "feel" that we are saved. A pastor might feel he is the most righteous of his church and yet be nearer to Hell than the drug-dealer. We know that we are saved in the same way that we know the sun is shining, even if it's a cloudy day. Always bear in mind that our fickle nature is subject to extreme variation second by second. Our emotions can be so unstable; they often fluctuate with no explicit relation to the circumstances at hand. If I were saved by feeling, I might be saved and condemned 100 times a day. More than that, who would be the one who is saved? The one who

---

[19] 1 Timothy 1:15-16

feels himself so wicked that he deserves death, thus understanding the true nature of Law and sin? Or the one who feels that they have been accepted by Christ, even though they have no concept of their true evil? If the promise of salvation is legitimized through emotion, then it is no promise at all. "Till death do us part" does not mean "unless I have lost my feelings for you."

Therefore, fear not, for your salvation is secure in Christ Jesus.

XII

The Sinner

As an additional resource to understand salvation, it might be beneficial to recount my first interactions, and subsequent salvation, with and in Christ using the analogy I have already set forth between the two warring cities of righteousness and sin.

I remember fighting for the emperor. It wasn't that long ago, actually. In fact, viewed in light of everlasting life, it seems like it was only mere seconds ago that I was fighting for the accuser. I was a competent soldier, signing up for and charging headfirst into all sorts of sin, but what made me most valuable to the emperor—who deserves no name—was my talent of sabotage. My outward allegiance to Christ, while being inwardly content to engage in transgression, provided an advantage to the master-tactician which was exploited often and accurately. My inward spirit of self did not reflect the outward words I preached of pledging myself to Christ. And, contrary to the presupposition of politicians, people aren't stupid. The acquaintances around me recognized that my spirit was the same as theirs (dead) and categorized Christian behavior to be synonymous with their secularism. Even though I refrained from partying and stayed away from the other stereotypical actions the Christian is not supposed to engage in, I would simply offer a half-smile and chuckle when my classmates told me what their planned "activities" for the evening were. By not replying with a Christian response, I was equipping them to justify their worldly behavior. Satan utilized my spiritual apathy to persuade the lost that their position before the Almighty God was the same as the saved.

Thankfully, the older I get, the less I remember the atrocities I committed against God during my service in Satan's empire. However, there was one particular battle I remember well. On the plains of the temporal, situated between horizons of eternity, I was in the thick of the war for souls. As the emperor heralded his orders from his safe-house at the rear of the battle to his kings and queens, commanding us to lie, steal, lust, and to hate, I came face-to-face with the enemy commander. I was initially surprised to see Him in the bloodiest area of the battle. For that matter, I was blown-away to see the extensive number of enemy officers and soldiers in the thickest part of the fight. It was the exact opposite of the hierarchy I was a part of; I was alone, fighting on my own.

In previous contemplations, I had come to accept the reality that the majority of our leaders were brutal in peace and cowardly in war, so seeing the Supreme fighting valiantly next to His poorest servant seemed incomprehensible to me. This commander did not attempt to hurt me, nor did He pronounce vengeance upon my soul. Even as I attempted to kill Him, swinging my sword of sin and death with all my power at His neck, He did not engage in my form of primitive combat. He weathered my every assault and never hurt me back.

After realizing that my numerous attempts to rid Him of life were futile, I relented and came spirit-to-spirit with Christ. At first, a deep sense of shame and sorrow engulfed my conscience like paper consumed by fire. I knew what side I was on, and it wasn't the right one. My previous sins disgraced me to no end. Initially, this only made me angrier.

I hoped, "Perhaps if He would just forget about me and leave me alone, these feelings would go away."

But He didn't leave, my feeling of guilt didn't go away, and my hatred for Him seemed to expand exponentially. I did not witness a being who was cruel and malevolent, but one who was and is undoubtedly the meekest person I have ever known and ever will know.

"Wasn't that a wonderful relief?" you exclaim. "To know that He had the ability to righteously wipe you out of existence and yet to keep His condemning sword sheathed?"

Ah! But in that moment of epiphany, I almost wished He was vengeful! Bering witness to His meekness, coupled with my hard heart, mocked me. And His refusal to end my life only seemed to compound my misery. My incorrect understanding of the nature of God and His character relegated His mercy to a kind of torment for my previous sin. Living with a haunted conscience appeared to be a fate worse than death. My pride could not co-exist with a man such as Christ, let alone serve Him.

As He pierced my heart with His purifying eyes of judgement, revealing my failure to achieve His standard of perfection, His physical sword remained sheathed. I capitulated, fell to my knees, both spiritual and physical, and cried, "Strike me down for I have abused Your eternal being!"

I can assure you, it is not a comfortable feeling when you admit to the man who is not just the apex of all things but also the being upon whom everything is contingent that you have treated Him with hostility and hatred. Interestingly, I concluded that I would never say such a thing under my own power; something must have already changed within me. Yet those feelings are dwarfed by the emotions of embarrassment that arise when you recognize that your facade, your pathetic attempt to manipulate Christ into thinking you loved

Him, was always known by Himself. The enlightenment of my foolishness reached its fulfilment when I understood that I hated Christ, and not only did I attempt to trick Him into believing I loved Him but I also had failed to realize that Christ, the one I despised, is the God of the Universe. For years, I had the audacity to try and pull the wool over the omniscient, omnipresent, and omnipotent being. Then I not only realize that I deserved death but I wanted it.

As I waited for judgement to be executed against me, I saw the image of the invisible God in this divine man. He was not what I expected. When I imagined the Infinite, the sovereign Creator over all seen and unseen reality, I thought of pomp and splendor beyond all comprehension. I expected such a God in a cosmic parade to showcase His limitless power to all creation, to pass through the Earth as one passes through a hamlet of 20 on a road trip. It is impossible to imagine how infinitesimally small and insignificant our world is compared to the grand scope of the Milky Way galaxy, let alone the universe. Why should a being of such magnitude even acknowledge our primal habitation, categorized as it is by wars and corruption? If he did, because of some mysterious rationalization, make contact with Earth, why subject us to anything kinder than complete, unquestionable servitude? Better yet, unless He is amused with our wars and suffering, which I now know

He is not, why not annihilate us angry, arrogant little creatures entirely?

If God did reveal Himself on Earth, as I now realized He did, it seemed obvious that He would be continually flanked by an incalculable number of angelic legions and spiritual servants. Granted, even those warriors who are unfathomably powerful, those whom the mind cannot comprehend, hardly seemed fitting for a king who controls time and space. Nonetheless, our customs of the day embed within our subconscious a preconception that extraordinary beings are required to display their power. With the person of Christ being revealed as God, I braced to hear, "Bow to me or be annihilated for I am king..." But I told you, God was not what I expected.

XIII

The Surprised

My imagination in describing His character could not have been further from the truth. Instead, when I met Christ, I saw a seemingly normal, ordinary man bow low before me and say, "I serve you, for I am your King."

My spirit could not comprehend. There was no display of grandeur, no arrogant behavior, and no armies advancing to dominate Earth and its sinful populous. He did not arrive on Earth with the stature of Adonis or with the tactical intentions of Napoleon. He did not indulge Himself with the glorious splendor of Solomon's riches—what, after all, is gold compared to the glory of the Lord? Instead, He presented Himself as a common man, ordinary and plain. There is, of course, nothing ordinary or plain about Him, for He is the Son of God.

In my prior attempts to assert my dominance over the written Law, I found myself stung and burned by its perfection. But with Christ, the Law welcomed and enveloped Him in the assurance of fulfilment from the Lord. I witnessed Him become one with the Law. The Law is Christ, and Christ is the Law. They combine and reveal themselves to be one and the same.

The moment His eyes pierced my soul, I realized all truth and knowledge are His and, as such, perfect justice is His alone to administer. All that I had done and all the sins I had committed flashed before my eyes, and I felt I should be immediately struck with the lightning of eternal damnation and sent straight to Hell. We are acutely aware in our regular lives that if we break the laws imposed upon us by our elected officials, we will face discipline. Therefore, it seemed to me self-evident that when a man such as I confessed his atrocities to the one Who is the Law, this Eternal Judge should destroy me with the word of His mouth. On the contrary, Christ looked at me with a kindness not finite, and I was blanketed with a love I cannot describe. Complementary with this blanket of peace was a promise from His mouth: "Your sins are forgiven."

I believe the truth of this most profound statement to be the greatest miracle in all reality of all time. God's creation of me, His continuing love while I was submersed in transgression, the Infinite becoming an infant, the submission of God in His sojourn as man, Christ's perfect life, surrender to death, eternal resurrection, and as a product of these miracles, the cleansing of my filthy sinful heart, the death of my old nature, and my first resurrection in Christ Jesus are all secured within the vault of this claim: "Your sins are forgiven."

Only after this epiphany did I understand that Jesus *is* also love. Jesus is love and love is Jesus. And if the law is a description of Jesus, then the law is a picture of love. I wondered how the Law could be a picture of love if it literally condemned me to death.

It is precisely because the Law condemns the sinner to die that it becomes a picture of the purest expression of love. The Law, sentencing the sinner to Hell, actually intends to reveal to man that Christ was selflessly required to lay down His life and endure Hell for us. The Law pointed to me, told me I could never measure up to the standard of righteousness, and then revealed that standard, Jesus. Christ needed to die for me, His enemy, in my place, thus precipitating a perfect love.

As I stood there at the conclusion of the battle, motionless and shocked by the statement, "Your sins are forgiven," I found myself in the peculiar position of being entirely unable to return to my now former empire. Instead, my feet ushered me to follow Christ into His camp. I had no disguise to dress in, and no stealth to infiltrate the camp. Instead, I came just as I was. I walked into the camp of the Commander through the front gate and was not welcomed with icy enmity or mocking sneers by those who already fought for Christ, but with friendly smiles, welcoming personalities, and loud rejoicing (for what reason, I did not yet know). I had never felt such united happiness and peace amongst a group of people.

XIV

The Substitute

The moment I entered that bastille of righteousness, I was immediately directed to the Infinite's court. It was at the center of the camp and surrounded by the most powerful warriors I had ever seen, yet no one but the judge was present beyond the court's entrance. As I walked through the gates, I looked down and lost track of how many open wounds of sin were littered on my body, and I dared not count the scars. I shuddered as I contemplated how broken and sinful my spirit must really be and concluded that if there was ever a man who deserved Hell, it was me. I expected nothing less than the judgement, "Damnation, forever!" But again, I was surprised. Though the path leading up to the Judge, who appeared distant, seemed interminable, I was brought before him in the blink of an eye. I expected to have more time to think of responses to His questions, to remember the good things I thought I had done, and to

The Substitute

try and hide my sins, but my journey ended in the blink of an eye.

However, throughout my whole walk toward the Judge, even if it did seem remarkably short, Christ stood right beside me. I did not go into that fateful court alone. My relief was evident when Christ did not stop at the door but continued on and even stood in front as I took my place in the dock.

When I realized such things, I remember wondering if my fate was going to be a paradox. I understood my situation to be exceedingly hopeless. Any attempt to conjure an excuse for my sin led to five other problems. As I tried to stall my impending doom, I thought, "As an ascribed sinner, I am absent of God and thereby evil. Instead, the god is me…but if the one true God is to save and be with me, I must become purified of my sin. For sin is lawlessness, and He is the Law. But this purification of sin would necessarily imply that I am no longer void of God, which must mean that God would live in me. But how can God live in me if I am presently a sinner?"

The answer, of course, is simple: ask Him. That is the miracle of salvation.

Before we went into the courtroom, we briefly stopped outside. In love, only a love that God Himself could possess, all of my wounds (my sins) were transferred over to Christ. He took my sin, my shame, my infirmities, my rebellion, my pride, my guilt, my failures and flaws, and placed them upon Himself. It was as though I became Christ and He became me. With His now-battered body, bruised and broken, He managed a humble smile and assured me all would soon be well. Together, we entered the courtroom. The Judge sat on His throne and emitted a light I cannot fathom. He saw Christ with all my sins and ruled according to the evidence presented. The wound of lying on my right arm was now on Jesus's right arm. The sin of self-righteousness on my left leg was now on Christ's left leg. The very sin itself—my separation from God and declaration that I alone am sufficient for life—consumed Christ. He hung His head low in shame, for even my guilt which used to torment me was transferred over to Him.

As I stood there, unsure of what to do, I heard Christ speak, "Tanner pleads not guilty. His sin has been committed to Me."

I looked at myself and saw that I was blameless. My wretched heart was clean! The Judge observed my being, recognized that I was blameless, and determined me innocent.

Christ was sentenced to death.

He received the entire fury of the punishment I deserve. In an instant, Christ experienced the eternity apart from the Father reserved for me. In a moment, He undertook Hell.

XV

The Saved

As I walked speechlessly out of the courtroom, I contemplated (and this should speak volumes of my human condition), "But if that's the end of it all, so what? If I am going to be removed from the camp or if I'm just going to return to fight for Satan and receive more sinful scars, what good is the substitute of Christ? To delay the inevitable? Of what use is His death? I already know I cannot keep the law, so living well will not justify me before the Father again...bugger! Certainly there are advantages of being cleansed of sin, but if my fate is, in the grand scheme of things, equal with Hitler's, Mao's, and Stalin's, I see no point in anything. A dead Christ is a failed Christ. And a failed Christ is a false Christ."

I become, paradoxically, a devoted follower of nihilism as I awaited the pit where all others have apparently gone before me. Instead of being grateful for being saved from death, I became pessimistic and distrusting of what should happen to me.

Therefore, it should be no surprise that my entire body tensed to attention when I heard the news that Christ was not dead, but alive. The Father found Christ to be righteous after paying the punishment for sin and raised Him from the dead!

The epiphany was clear, and unlike my sinful actions, I shall never forget this moment. If Christ, my substitute, took my sin and guilt at His sentencing and death, it was as though He became me. And if it is as though he became me, it is as though I myself died and paid the punishment for my sin. This sacrifice pays the price of my sin, true, but I also know that sin is the absence or separation of God. Christ paid that penalty for me, but I am still separated from God! I am still in sin. Scripture states that, as a Christian, my punishment has been paid, my debt has been cleared, and I am a "free" man. Yet this freedom is worth nothing if I am still dead. A savior might open the gate for a prisoner, but if the prisoner is deceased, what good is the salvation? Therefore, I must be reconciled or no longer separated from God to be sinless. I must accept the sacrifice of Christ; I need to ask Him into my heart. Yet if Christ is dead, how can I ask Him to live in my heart? Can a mortal who is alive call a dead man to himself? But because Christ was raised from the dead, He lives forever. If He is alive, then He can live in my being!

I then thanked Christ for His salvation and asked Him into my heart and again thought, "Since Christ has been raised from the dead, I too have been raised from the dead. Christ not only lives in me, but because He is God and the author of life, He also *gives* life to me. Thus, because I have been raised from the dead, I have life. If I have life, I am free from death forever and thus, free from sin. Because I have been raised from the dead, death can never hold me in slavery again. A prison with an open gate is useless. In the same way, Hell's gates have been demolished, and Christ ushered me out of torment and into Heaven. Therefore, being free from sin and Hell, I am welcomed to be with God for eternity in perfection, because I am justified in Jesus." It was then that I became a resurrected man.

That is the wonder of the Gospel.

XVI

The Scared

But in some indeterminate location not yet experienced by mortal men, there is another courtroom whose doors are waiting to be opened. Above the entrance of this great finality hangs a sign that says, "THE DAMNED." Many men and women, great and small, young and old, have lined up outside the court and are awaiting their fateful sentence. How is judgement pronounced? I do not know. But I do know that the Christian is not with them. He will never enter that dreadful room where the screams of sinners, where the weeping of the wicked, and where the hopeless cries of the condemned are forever silenced behind that impenetrable door welded shut with the pride of the sinner.

XVII

The Secure

Contrast that horrible fate (we shall discuss it more later) with the Christian. I no longer worry about my eternity! I no longer fear sin! The debt has been paid! Christ now protects me, cares for me, and ensures I am not destroyed by my enemy, Satan.

Observe the devoted husband. Watch how vigilantly he protects his wife from those who would do her harm. With absolute determination and strength, he will protect her at any cost; his life is laid down both metaphorically and perhaps physically for her. Any intruder who dares imitate even a very calculated strategic move against her is met with unrivalled ferocity. He keeps her safe, for it is his duty to do so, and he is dishonored if he shies away from such responsibility.

The Christian is the bride of Christ. Jesus is the captain of my soul, and seeing the face of my Savior in me, viruses, wars, suffering, tribulations, and death itself slink back into the abyss from which they came. I am not autonomous, thank heavens, but free in my Lord. And now, dear reader, if you are in Christ, you are forever free, too.

XVIII

The Gradual Liberation

In my unsaved state, I am a man of lawlessness. But I am saved. Thus, in me, a former man of lawlessness, the lawful one lives so that I might be freed from the burden of the Law and live because the Law is fulfilled in me, making me a man of the Law.

But we must be precise. When I say that I am no longer a man of lawlessness, I am only referring to my spirit. Presently, my body continues to decay and is still subject to sin. Because it is a sinful body, it is a lawless body. The two halves of my duality, my spirit and body, are currently locked in a civil war jostling for dominance. Though they are engaged in fierce combat, they begrudgingly stay united because they know that each half is incomplete without the other. If they were forced to be divorced from each other, existence would become like a loving husband forced to be separated from his wife. Life would become altogether undesirable because it requires both spirit and body to be fulfilled.

In their desire for conquest over the other, my spirit draws its power from the new Law and my body draws from the old. Although it will not always be this way—my body will be resurrected and happily made anew so that both it and the spirit will be completely under the Law of Christ—for the moment, I am forced to engage in a continual battle with sin as my body tries to be evil and my spirit tries to keep the evil at bay.

Upon initial assessment, the odds of winning this battle appear to be weighted heavily in favor of the body. Although we are now members of Christ's country, we are required to infiltrate the City of Sin and live among the lost as witnesses. But in that city, the Christian spirit is surrounded by fallen people, serving a fallen emperor, and living in a fallen physical city. We are quickly reminded that this place is where sin is not only inevitable but is perversely natural. Of course, the body is right at home, but our spirit groans, wishing to be back with the Lord.

All around him, the disciple witnesses the unbearable weight of the Law crushing man into dust. Its intricate rules and immense regulations which once scorched us under the gaze of a holy God now suffocate our unsaved neighbors. Every crack, every corner, and every abode is rife with sin. There is nowhere physical to hide. All the while, the body is like a child waiting to ride a rollercoaster as it proclaims, "We're next! We're next! We're next in line to sin!" The spirit is like the motion-sick parent trying to persuade the child to go on something more benign, like the bumper-cars.

Tragically, after an extended period of time in this hostile land, it is very common to hear of a Christian's capitulation to the gods of the world. Although he is saved by Christ, the Christian is still in bondage to the Law. Instead of fixing their eyes on Jesus as the fulfillment of the scriptures, the struggling Christian returns to gaze at the banner of the Law. What happens next is entirely expected.

For example, the Law says, "Thou shall not commit adultery."[20] Instantly, your body craves adultery and you capitulate to your body's desire for sin. You recognize the law not to commit adultery, but then go home, commit adultery, feel horribly wicked after the action, become tragically depressed, try to cheer yourself up through pleasure, and repeat the cycle for what seems to be *ad infinitum*. Of course, after repeatedly engaging in this struggle, you find yourself unable to quit. Hemingway said that a man goes bankrupt in two ways: gradually and then suddenly. The same is true for addiction to sin.

The subsequent strategy of Satan is to accuse. "Sinner! How can God love you? You pathetic, immoral, evil, vile little creature."

---

[20] Exodus 20:14

Inevitably, in your own estimation, the Father of Lies seems to be a liar no longer.

"He's right. How can God love me?" I am undeserving of kindness, and I despise myself. My lust, which I have engaged in, has become a hydra and is one whom I cannot slay. It is a beast that only grows in power with each passing day. Though I hate it, I feed it and feel its control rising over me. What a vicious cycle of remorse and relapse.

I do not know my fate.

My salvation is in question, I think, and so I return to that demon of lust for relief. Then I go to the Christian circle for help, perhaps to the church, and I am told, "Recruit an accountability partner, throw away your phone and your computer, you must have more faith, and you must pray harder." They say, "Don't handle, don't taste, don't touch!"[21] These pieces of advice are supposed to barricade my body from committing sin. And so I do the things commanded. I pray, "Oh, my God, my God, free me from this wretched evil. How I pray that You would take this sin away. Kill me if I sin like this again. I'll do anything to make it stop." And all I receive is deafening silence. Perhaps I do not have enough faith. Perhaps I am not saved at all.

This situation is not an outlier on the human distribution. This is not an anomaly. On the contrary, based on the testimony of the numerous high school and

---

[21] Colossians 2:20-23

university students I have become acquainted with, this epidemic has become the norm. The advice that is commonly given to the desperate souls hoping to combat such sin is rarely effective because it treats the symptoms and not the cause.

Suppose I am iron deficient. Without a blood test, I cannot know that I am iron deficient, but I know that I'm not feeling well. So I go to the doctor and tell him my symptoms: "I am extraordinarily tired and very weak. My skin is quite pale, and I just don't feel that well."

If he is a very foolish doctor, he will say, "Well, get some more sleep for your tiredness. Begin lifting weights to combat your weakness. Get some sun to tan your skin, and take an Ibuprofen to feel better."

Such a doctor is only treating my symptoms and not the disease. Even if I do all the things he has prescribed, I will still be low on iron, and the products of that deficiency, the tiredness and weakness, will continue. I must be given iron supplements to cure my ailment, and when I take them, the symptoms of deficiency will cease.

The same story is true when we try to cure the symptoms of sin and not the sin itself. Our proposed "remedies" are no remedies at all, and the worldly advice we administer deteriorates as it is utilized. Can an accountability partner save you? Can an internet filter save you? Does throwing away your phone eliminate the sin within you? Does finding purpose in your life cure you of your evil ways? Can an intellectual, even a very brilliant one, freely administer salvation? Perhaps your mentor can give outward physical advice on how to withstand cravings for a little while, but can they say, "Your sins against God have been forgiven"? By no means!

Yet just because none of these proposed ideas are saviors, does not mean they hold no value. In *conjunction* with Christ and with Christ alone as the leader, these barricades can be purposed to help mortify sin in the body.

But sin, like the emperor, is merciless. If the filter alone is relied upon, the sinful actions *will* return. We are not stupid, are we? Does sin see a blocked site and go, "Oh well. Guess I'll tempt someone else. This filter is clearly too strong to outmaneuver"?

No. Sin is crafty and brilliant, and if a general does not give his enemy due respect, he is doomed. Oh certainly, the filter might block the explicitly explicit sites, but soon an ad will arise on a supposedly clean site, or a friend will show you a sinful video, and so on. The more you rely on a filter to save you, the weaker it becomes.

I am not telling you an accountability partner is useless or not to listen to the intellectual. But on their own, these barricades against evil, even if placed with the tactical genius of Nelson, will be easily defeated by sin. Why? They will be destroyed because sin does not need to sneak around a barricade; it does not need to annihilate it, or break it, or crush it into dust. It does not need to do any of these things because, just as Satan was in the Garden of Eden with Adam and Eve, sin is already behind the walls. The true weakness in trying to remove ourselves from the world is that the world is already in us. Defensive walls do not change the cleanliness of the city. What then is the cure?

Christ is the cure! He alone eliminates sin. He alone says, "Your sins are forgiven."[22] He alone cures our disease of sin. Why then are we trying to cure something that, by definition, no longer rules the Christian?

Therefore, the way to stop sinning is to realize you don't have to stop sinning! Look only to Christ, for He is the salvation. Whether we sin 1, 100, or 10^x times, this axiom will never change. Christ has taken the evil and its necessary punishment away. The sin has been destroyed, and what remains, the products of sin that you and I still engage in, are nothing more than the lingering effects of our previous affliction. That is the secret—although it was never intended to be a secret—to cease habitual sin. Worry about it no longer! Do not fear losing your salvation. If you could lose it, it would already be lost.

In your prayers, contemplations, and everyday life, do not dwell on your previous embarrassment, shame, and depression because of how you sinned. Instead, focus on Christ, who He is, how He saved you, how much He loves you, and what He is presently doing. In this, you will observe a gradual desire to cease sinning.

---

[22] Luke 5:20

"Yes, but I heard Mrs. W using very foul language yesterday. Surely she cannot expect me to believe that she is saved."

"Is she a Christian?"

"She is."

"Then she is freed from the condemning Law and is saved."

"Maybe. But I caught Mr. E watching explicit videos the other day. He admitted he's addicted and has watched thousands of videos. His salvation must be in question."

"Is he a Christian?"

"He is."

"Then Christ has paid the punishment for Mr. E's sin! He is therefore freed from the law and is saved in Jesus."

"But I…"

"Freed."

"Ah, but he…"

"Freed."

Now, when discussing this kind of freedom, I mean it in the common, modern sense—freedom as the ability to act without fear of condemnation or punishment. If I, a Christian man who has chosen to abstain from alcohol, decides to drink a gallon of whiskey every day for the rest of my life and live in a perpetual state of drunkenness, I would remain righteous in the eyes of God. If, as a product of excessive drink, I became harsh, course, mean, and abusive, as long as I have placed my faith in Christ, I shall be counted as righteous as Moses, Paul, and Christ himself. This is because Jesus lives in me, and I am free from condemnation in Him. My salvation is not derivative of my works but is a product of Jesus' existence in my heart. That is the sort of freedom we are presently talking about. All my punishment incurred from living in drunkenness is paid for by Jesus, and so the penalty cannot be applied to me.

But the prudent, yet well-meaning Christian might be apprehensive about accepting this concept of freedom in Christ as doctrine. Although sin always comes at a price, "There may be," he says, "a possible temptation to go ahead and sin freely." His mind, upon contemplation of what I am proposing, might conclude, "Christians now have free reign to open casinos, smoke drugs, watch explicit videos…do whatever they want! If we are free from condemnation, who cares what we do?"

Or the equally as prudent, yet self-righteous Christian (the one who has that remarkable ability to keep every aspect of the outward Law) might decry this doctrine of freedom twice as loud as anyone else. On the grounds of traditional biblical interpretation, the legalist and moralist might despise such a belief because it "makes a repulsive mockery of the Christian faith by cheapening works and good actions engaged in post-salvation. After all," they argue, "James says that faith without works is dead."

The concern present in both parties, although originating from different references, arrives at the same conclusion: "To say you are free to do whatever you want after salvation promotes sinful living."

If our only definition of freedom is to act without fear of discipline from authorities, then perhaps this objection is legitimate. But we must recognize another consequence of this newfound liberation from slavery.

When I say "freedom," I do *not* mean autonomy. In fact, from the very controversial perspective of scripture, human autonomy is not freedom or reward, but is slavery and punishment. On the contrary, we are created to be "free servants," and when we divert from that purpose, chaos erupts.

What I am really talking about when I say "freedom" is the absolute alignment of each individual will in both spirit and body. As it stands, my spirit wants to serve God, but my body does not. Although I am free, I am not yet *entirely* free, because these two entities are at war with each other. Thus, my ability to do what I truly want is diminished. My spirit says, "Do not lie!" and my body says, "Lie!"

So, when I talk about "freedom in Christ," I actually mean, "My new spirit being given a power that allows it to take the sinful body under control. Because my sinful body is being brought under the jurisdiction of the spirit, I can more freely do what God wants me to do." Therefore, the "Christian" who argues, "I am free to do

The Gradual Liberation

whatever I want because the Law has been fulfilled in me," is arguing an oxymoron. A walking contradiction. A logical impossibility. He is like a cube that rolls or a vertical bed, for he preaches to both love and hate Christ simultaneously.

Recall the heroic rally of General Norman Cota at Omaha Beach during the invasion of Normandy during World War II. That hellish beach was littered with tragedy and horror unthinkable to a typical conscience. As the soldiers were being slaughtered by the Nazis, Cota arrived and exuded a leadership that forced his men to follow. But they are not forced out of fear. They are not coerced to fight for Cota because he is pointing a gun at their heads or is holding their family hostage. Instead, they are forced to fight for him because of who he is and what he is doing. Cota had such a magnetic quality that no solider could resist following him into the storm of war.

I daresay that the soldiers under Cota are not forced to fight at all, but rather, they become free to. Before the general arrived, the beach was not so much a battlefield as it was a sandy strip of slaughter. When Cota came, he organized the men and led them to their objectives. The soldiers could now fight as intended because they have a leader giving them encouragement and direction.

In the same light, the soldier in the army of Christ does not fight because his master is harsh, but because He is not. The Christian does not stop sinning because he is afraid of losing Christ, but because Christ can never be lost.

My sinful nature parleys, "Then let us engage in sin for the rest of our earthly lives. When eternity knocks at our door, we will get to live with Christ in Heaven forever. It would be the best of both worlds!"

How could I do such a thing? Sin killed my Christ! The Christian is, by definition, the one who hates sin, for he has renounced it in repentance. When I am questioned, "You are free in Christ, so do you not have the freedom to sin?" I answer, "I do! But because I am free in Christ, I do not want to, and therefore, I will not!" Like the soldier who is free to fight as planned, freedom is the newfound ability to say "no" to my evil desires.

Christian, sin in your life has been killed. Sin in you is dead because Christ lives in you, and He is life. And if something is dead, it no longer holds power over anything. You and I no longer fear Stalin or Nero, because they are decaying in the grave. So too, if sin has been killed within us, its power is eliminated. If its power has been removed, then we no longer need to capitulate to evil. Therefore, since Christ died for our sin, we have been freed from the Law. But because we are freed from the Law, we do not continue to break the Law. Rather, we now uphold the Law in Christ. And one day, when my body is made immortal, both its will and the will of my spirit will be perfectly in harmony. The civil war inside me will end, and I will never experience such conflict again. *That* is true freedom.

XIX

The Destiny of the Dead

The emperor, his lackeys, and the City of Sin will soon be sentenced—decimated, destroyed, and vanquished by the breath of Christ. Satan recognizes this. Already, his armada is steadily sinking deeper into the depths of the abyss. His personal dreadnaught is teetering on unsteady edges as the Admiral of Heaven closes in for the killing barrage. From the horizon, the Accuser sees the navy of righteousness steam forward with full force. His only ploy is to sink as many other boats as possible out of spite for Jesus. The hatred of Lucifer is realized in attempting to destroy and drag down every soul he can into Hell with him. Repent! Sail away and toward Christ!

But what if you don't? What is the punishment for those who reject the Eternal God and His salvation while on Earth? Exactly that—an eternity without God and His salvation. This is *Hell*.

The Destiny of the Dead

The servant of self, the self-appointed god, and the one who has rejected Christ has been determined guilty. The word "Forever" now hangs on a sign above his cell that is locked from the inside.

Suppose you commit the unforgivable sin of rejecting the salvation of Heaven freely offered by Jesus Christ and then die alone. After the dreadful trial at the Great White Throne of Judgment and your subsequent sentence of everlasting death, you begin to descend into Hell. As your acceptance of the reality that there are no second chances begins to take effect, you start to feel the Lake of Fire below seething and churning with the unbearable heat of your iniquity. However, the flames of Hell are not colored crimson. They are not a blueish white, either. The flames produce heat unquenchable, but they emit no light. They generate no visible energy because this place violates all known laws of physics. In fact, nothing about Hell is natural. Everything feels wrong, chaotic, and perverted. What used to be familiar is now foreign, what used to be simple is now impossible, and what used to be joyful is now hated.

Desperately, assuming there is such a thing as an objective bearing in Hell, you look up, down, left, right, anywhere at all for even the smallest island constructed out of your good works. "If only the smallest bit of my body could be saved from this sea of shadowed flames!"

You find none. All you see is the fading light of God's glory glowing dimmer and dimmer. There will be no respite from this agony, ever. As your feet begin to sear from the uninhabitable molten you are now forced to call your home, you again frantically look all around. "Perhaps there is someone else here. Maybe I will suffer with them, and my misery will be eased."

For suffering, although uncomfortable, is comforted when you suffer with an acquaintance. But in Hell, there is no comfort. You find that you are alone. There is nobody. No one to see, nobody to hear, nobody to talk to, and nobody to interact with. As your head slips beneath the surface, the surface you cannot see, your being is so contracted with pain that a normal body would break and disintegrate.

After what seems like an eternity, but has only been seconds, you cry, "Perhaps I will drown and die. Then this suffering will end."

You do not. Instead, you are left to suffer, gasping for air in the flames of unrepentant sin for eternity. Lonely and forgotten by all, forever.

But nothing is so insufferable as the thought of asking for forgiveness. The mere concept of repentance makes you vomit. What an unthinkable alternative! You conclude, "It is better to suffer eternally for the empire I fought for my entire earthly life than to ask for forgiveness and live with the Trinity in glory."

Just as the Christian is experiencing true freedom in Heaven because his soul and body are perfectly united, the sinner is freed too. His body and soul are also in complete unification, but for a different reason. They are in a hellish harmony. Where there used to be conscience and natural law, all that is left of their duality is a vehement hatred for God. Both the unsaved body and soul are unending in their absolute purpose of detesting the Creator. Everything that used to be good in them is gone. The qualities and traits which made us love, cherish, and respect them have been destroyed. Their wisdom, beauty, and humor have all been lost as they have attained their true goal, the elimination of Jesus Christ in their life. All those who have chosen this tragic eternity proclaim, "Better to be a king or queen suffering forever alone than to serve Christ for even a second in perfection." If you cast yourself into Hell to escape God, then forever shall you stay.

But who can adequately describe this horrible existence? It is a reality so evil, wicked, painful, arrogant, depressing, and lonely, that no human experience, no matter how tragic, will ever compare.

Before we continue, it might be beneficial first to describe what Hell is *not*. It is not, as so many of us understand it to be, a physical place where Satan sits on his throne as king of sin and rules over the damned. In fact, I know I may have just described it as such, but Hell is not Hell because of its physical location and physical attributes. I merely utilized the imagery of flames searing the body to describe the torment of an eternity without God because Christ did the same. Granted, the state of being separated from God takes place in a physical location that we call "Ghenna" or "Hell" to avoid confusion, but it is not the geographical location that makes it horrible. In fact, I doubt very earnestly that Hell will be anything like I described. It will be worse.

It is fascinating that so many individuals conceptualize Hell as one big party rife with alcoholism, drugs, and other sensual pleasures the sinful soul enjoys. "At the very worst," they think, "it might be a little hot and crowded." Although an increasingly popular belief, I do not believe the one who has death clawing at their heart's door is comforted by such hopes. Few mortals preparing for the grave are at peace knowing they are going to Hell. But assuming pleasure can exist without God, if such a place is as sensual and pleasurable as the young crowd claims it to be, shouldn't they be excited to go? Why is there a longing in the heart to stay away from that place?

I think the main reason that many unbelievers hold to this view of Hell is because of how the Christian church has defined sin over the past decades. If we continue to talk about sin as though it is "the bad things we do," unbelievers are prone to believe that is all damnation will consist of. Logically, they believe that Hell, a sinful place, will be filled with "sinful" actions. Because the church has denounced the fruit of sin, like lust and gluttony, and not the root of sin (yourself), the unsaved believe "eternal suffering" is filled with the fruit of sin and not the root.

What then is Hell? It is where man is exalted in his own glory, but the exaltation of man is not at all glorious, but hideous. It is the state of being where you and everything around you are totally and completely void of God. That is not to say that the condemned are void of knowledge, individuality, or personality, but that they are void of *life*. It is to be void of life because the Infinite God is life. Therefore, life is intended to be eternal. The rejection of salvation is the rejection of God. The rejection of God is sin. Sin is the state of falling short of the glory of the Infinite. To fall short of the Infinite is to fall short of life. Falling short of life, is death. Therefore, Hell *is* a state of separation. It is the unthinkable reality of being separated from God forever, which is a conscious, everlasting, death.

But why forever? A loving parent does not discipline his or her child indefinitely, but only for a moment. A quick, precise punishment is usually all that is required to adequately correct a misbehaving child. And if God is our Father, why should our judgement be any different in terms of length? Why isn't purgatory a logical punishment (aside from the fact that it is never mentioned in scripture)?

Recall our previous discussion of wages and their obligation to be administered. Remember that a wage is not a form of charity but is a legitimate contract that requires workers to be compensated for selling their time. This is simply an extension of the "eye for an eye" doctrine of God's Law. A worker gives an employer some amount of labor and intellect, both encased in a measurement of time, and the employer compensates that trade with an equivalent amount of value in the form of cash. In the same way, the just Law requires a perfectly balanced punishment relative to the offence. And as we said before, an eye for a life is not fair.

If the punishment for unrepentant sin, Hell, is not infinite, then undesirable consequences logically follow. The first consequence is that the Law is not perfectly righteous and so Christianity disintegrates, because the righteous Law demands an eternal punishment. The Law becomes a fraud, the scriptures a fraud, and Christ a fraud. For the second consequence, suppose that the Law actually is just, but doesn't require an eternal punishment. Then the God who gave that Law is not an infinite being and is therefore created. Again, Christianity disintegrates and so does the philosophical definition of "God." So, transgression against God, who by definition is the uncreated being who has identical essence and existence, must delegate an infinite punishment in order to satisfy the righteous requirement of the Law. The wages of sin is only fulfilled if Hell is eternal with no chance of escape.

It is for that reason the Christian cannot ascribe to the doctrine of "repentance after death"—not only because the perfect scriptures state that repentance after death is impossible but because it is illogical. This just punishment, and absolute promise of God, cannot cease halfway through its administration, lest the wage becomes unjust and God untrue. If God declares that "it is appointed unto men once to die, but after this the judgment,"[23] then if a man has rejected God in this life, there cannot be mercy for him post-mortem. There is certainly the opportunity for mercy to be accepted in *this* life, and that translates to the eternal, but the opportunity for the damned to receive mercy, post-judgment, is a tragic fantasy. The spiritual signed contract will only be completed at the end of eternity. But because the Creator has no conclusion and, by definition, neither does eternity, then the horror of Hell must be everlasting.

Never forget that no one will descend so deep into the suffering of Hell as the Devil. He will not rule with an iron scepter nor will he dictate torture to the unsaved. He will be nothing more than a worm, thrown into the fire to shrivel up and yet never die. Satan might be called a lion on Earth, but he is little more than a kitten compared to the Lion of Judah. His fate will reflect as such.

---

[23] Hebrews 9:27

XX

The Ascension of the Alive and the Descension of the Divine

In direct contrast to Satan's sinking fleet, Heaven's battleships are sailing ahead at full speed.[24] The Admiral of all things, flanked by numerous escorts, has charted a course for the eternal plane while leaving the wicked behind. Nothing, not even death, can sink this convoy.

We have already answered the question of what will happen to those who reject the salvation of God. But what is the reward for those who *believe* in the salvation of the Eternal God? Again, exactly that—an eternity with God and His salvation. This is *Heaven*.

---

[24] Scripture presents the events of Heaven as having logical order set within time. I have chosen to instead describe these events as occurring almost simultaneously, but I have only done so for the sake of brevity. The way scripture describes life after our bodily death as existing in time is the only description to declare true.

The Ascension of the Alive and the Descension of the Divine

At the end of your life as the eyes begin to fade, the heart begins to strain, and as the family begins to cry, there is a voice. It is unmistakable and authoritative as you hear, "Come up here! Quickly! Here are your escorts, my angels, to help you on your journey."

Christian, this is the beginning of your reward. Every believer, at the moment of their salvation, was born-again; they are a new creation. Being "born-again" implies a family, and that family is the Trinity. You have been adopted into sonship and are already a child of God. Because the Christian is forever a child of the Divine, all of us are co-heirs with Christ. What is Christ's is now the Christian's. You inherit, among other things too wonderful for a sinful mind to comprehend, the estate allotted to Jesus: eternal life.

As you ascend into the City of God, leaving behind trials and tribulations, going above the sky, the stars, and the court of the Divine Council, a joyful smile assumes command of the countenance as you realize there is no need for second chances. Slowly, but steadily, you begin to comprehend that the Kingdom of Peace is yours. Similar to the unbeliever, the word "Forever" hangs above the city of this new dominion, but this is not a self-locking cell in Hades. Seeing the word "Forever" does not invoke a sense of dread for the Christian but of relief. It soothes old sores and invites all believers with the unforgettable and wonderful warmth of Christ. The nagging desire to sin, to declare thyself God, has vanished from your body and soul. The physical wounds that used to anguish and corrupt are mended; the mental and emotional afflictions which tormented the consciousness are forgotten. All the while this has been happening, you are being enveloped in a love and acceptance you have never experienced before and intrinsically know you will never lose.

The Citizen of Heaven is not afraid of what is to come but is joyfully anticipatory. There is an electric excitement that hums throughout the refined air as your eyes focus on one man—the Lord Jesus Christ. He is altogether a most brilliant surprise. For although you knew Him, you never really *knew* Him. Not completely anyway—sin made sure of that. It is only with the destruction of the mortal body and with its subsequent resurrection clothed in immortality that Jesus can be fully known.

Seeing His face makes you chuckle as you remember the misconstrued importance of good works, money, health…anything really. After seeing Christ for the first time and every time after that, it is evident that *nothing* could ever hold a candle to Him and His glory. Although certainly not unwelcome, it is all the more surprising and humbling when Christ personally calls you by name to formally legitimize your justification in front of the Father. Though you were previously inclined to nervousness, wondering if there wouldn't be at least some uncertainty regarding your eternal fate due to your sin, there is now none. All salvation is secure in Christ. He has promised everlasting and eternal life to those who believe in Him, and He cannot break His promises.

Instead, when you are brought before that grand court, you are rewarded for all the good things you did on Earth. That time you led a man or woman to Christ, quietly gave money to the poor, sacrificed much to raise your children, and honored your parents is recounted and all are rewarded. The Cherubim surrounding the throne of God clap and shout, "Congratulations! Well done, well done!" Christ is among them heaping you with praise and honor, though He deserves all of it, and the sounds of the orchestra erupt from the chamber, declaring the introduction of a sealed member of the heavenly family.

After that, you turn around and finally catch a glimpse of the physical realm of Heaven. The wonder of this place is not due to how foreign it is, but how normal it feels. As you walk with Christ, talking and joking together, the sheer magnitude of the wonder of the new Eden causes even your perfect senses to nearly overload from incomprehension. All around is the most brilliant architecture. Buildings constructed with a modern, apex-style design in one section, cozy log cabins and quaint farmhouses in another. Lush parks and gardens filled with vines and plants and flowers with colors and qualities previously concealed to the imperfect eye. Their fragrance fills the heights of Heaven with a clean scent of renewal, but sometimes such freshness is overcome by the smell of bakeries. The aroma of fresh breads, cakes, doughnuts, cookies, and other pastries often cascade through the streets of gold as food is prepared for the barbeques, banquets, and dinner parties that all will be a part of.

But, of course, the bakers must find their flour somewhere. You have been so interested and invested in learning of your eternal home that you failed to notice how far you had already gone. As you near the country, the farms become visible. Innumerable fields of every grain for all walks of life are being harvested in Heaven. Oats for the animals, wheat for the bakers, canola for oil, and so on. Farmers gather around their combines and hold one of life's finest pleasures—harvest meals in the field—together as a united group and proud of their work. We, the new rulers of Heaven, work up an appetite, for there is much work to be done. It is never the drudgery that we are accustomed to today, but a joyful work of ever-serving Christ. For this reason, the combines are continually running. After all, what could be more fulfilling for a farmer than providing the food that Christ Himself will eat? Or what could bring someone more joy than ensuring a child who starved to death on Earth shall never go hungry again?

As you return to the inner-city, you and Jesus decide to explore a university. All members speak with an enlightened dialect, brimming with kindness and

The Ascension of the Alive and the Descension of the Divine

happiness; these intellects speak with eloquence unparalleled. As you pass "Professor Lewis'" office, you recognize the voices of Solomon, Augustine, and Paul as they discuss over a cup of coffee the nature of God. With smiles, they invite you in, but you politely decline as there is still more to explore. It is not two steps down the hall that the contemplations of Newton, Leibniz, and Lennox are clear, proving the new maths that have been revealed. I earnestly hope to see people like Dr. Jordan Peterson, Ben Shapiro, and Sir Roger Penrose among them.

The sweet sound of Britain's Christianity entices you to open the auditorium doors and listen to Reverend C.H. Spurgeon preach to angels and humans about the wonder of the Lord they can finally see. His voice, as sweet as it was reported to be, is amplified with his resurrected body. The sinful vocal chords of the old Earth, no matter how sanctified, never possessed the capacity to speak in such a way. Somewhere else, Corrie Ten Boom and Dietrich Bonhoeffer are describing how the Lord comforted them in the depths of Nazi persecution. Standing beside both heroes, their new brother and friend, the former Nazi General, Wilhelm Keitel, is joyfully recounting how Christ granted forgiveness to him before his execution at Nuremberg. Though such testimonies are stunning, there are other people to meet.

What about the motel maid who cleaned rooms for 30 years? She was actually a scientific genius, but could never acquire the necessary capital to attend school. It is no matter in Heaven, for where there used to be scarcity, there is now none. The beautiful equations that cram the chalkboard are now available to all. She is sitting at the front of the class, quickly becoming a master of her field in quantum physics or topological math.

As the downtown lights being to sparkle with the introduction of evening (if there is such a thing in eternity), Christ, knowing your interest in the classical arts, introduces you to the orchestra. All attendees dress their very best, and the concert begins. Songs that praise God are played with the greatest passion and the most fervent joy. Harmonies the sinful ear could never hear are now listened to by all.

But what if your personality is not inclined to enjoy these things? I only utilized these examples because I myself enjoy them, but what about you, dear reader?

I also love muscle cars, and maybe you do too. Can there not also be a drag strip where the finest drag cars are pitted against each other on a nightly basis? Perhaps you have a love for dance. I do not, but that is certainly not to say there won't be the most elegant recital halls in Heaven. Or what about sports? Hockey, baseball, volleyball, football, badminton—a fierce but fun competitiveness will be present between the teams.

But certainly my thinking is too limited. Our sinful mind and the sheer brilliance of God's design refuses to allow us to imagine the true nature of Heaven. It is so much more than the mind I can fathom. All my examples are an insufficient description.

Regardless, Heaven is not beautiful because of its architecture or buildings or things which are inanimate. It is not beautiful because of gold streets or crystal water, though they are stunning to behold. On the contrary, Heaven is beautiful because old friendships separated on Earth are reunited for eternity. It is beautiful because death and mourning and crying and pain are forgotten. It is beautiful because old inefficiencies in the mind invoked by that demon of Alzheimer's or dementia are wiped away. It is beautiful because veterans cutoff by the horror of war are now in perfect peace and aborted children are now showing their forgiven parents around the city. It is beautiful because of the people that are there. It is beautiful, only because of Christ.

Nothing compares to being with Jesus. If Hell is the state of being totally absent from God, then Heaven must be the state of being totally united with God. And this is the fundamental point I should like to hammer home. Heaven is not a place; it's a person! Heaven is the person of Jesus Christ.

Why? Classically, Heaven has been defined as "the dwelling place of God." Let us then say that where God lives is where we rightfully call "Heaven." Now, as scripture declares, God was and is in Christ Jesus. Thus, Heaven is Christ. And because Christ Jesus lives in the believer, the believer becomes the temple or dwelling place of God. The Kingdom of Heaven is within the Christian. Therefore, and this is the wonder of it all, when a believer accepts Christ, he does not ascend to Heaven, but Heaven descends and lives in him! As we iterated in the previous chapter, the physical city of Heaven, filled with all its awe and splendor, would be Hell if Christ were not there with us. I could be in space, in the desert, on a planet light-years away, or in a modern metropolis, and as long as I am with my Christ, I am in Heaven.

That is why it took so long to see the city—you were too busy focusing on Jesus. And that is not a bad thing. We could continue this discussion, but I fear the book would never end. So let us avoid our continual mistake of thinking little of Heaven and expecting even less. On the contrary, think much of that soon-to-be beautiful existence and expect even more.

About the Author

Tanner Hnidey is a Canadian Lay-Preacher, Bible Teacher, and a veteran of Bible Camp ministry. He has taught numerous students and campers of various ages, everything from the fundamentals of Christianity to the prophecies of Revelation. In order to better understand how people in a fallen world make decisions, Tanner earned a degree in Economics, with a concentration in Industrial Organization, from the University of Calgary. In his spare time, Tanner enjoys studying scripture, speaking about Christ, and hauling grain on the farm. Tanner lives in Alberta, Canada. Look for him on Instagram, Twitter, Facebook, and Youtube!

Manufactured by Amazon.ca
Bolton, ON